Data Protection

for voluntary organisations

Second edition

Paul Ticher

DIRECTORY OF SOCIAL CHANGE   in association with
Bates, Wells & Braithwaite

Published by
Directory of Social Change
24 Stephenson Way
London NW1 2DP
Tel. 020 7209 5151; Fax 020 7391 4804
e-mail: books@dsc.org.uk
website: www.dsc.org.uk
from whom further copies and a full publications list are available.

Directory of Social Change is a Registered Charity no. 800517

First published 2000
Second edition 2002

ISBN 1 903991 19 6

British Library Cataloguing in Publication Data
A catalogue record for this book is available from the British Library

Cover design by Linda Parker
Text designed by Sarah Nicholson
Typeset by Tradespools Ltd., Frome
Printed and bound by Antony Rowe Ltd, Chippenham, Wiltshire

Other Directory of Social Change departments in London:
Courses and conferences 020 7209 4949
Charity Centre 020 7209 1015
Charityfair 020 7209 1015
Publicity 020 7391 4900
Research 020 7391 4880

Directory of Social Change Northern Office:
Federation House, Hope Street, Liverpool L1 9BW
Courses and conferences 0151 708 0117
Research 0151 708 0136

Contents

Acknowledgements

The author would like to thank all those who have contributed to the book, especially those participants on training courses and briefing sessions whose acute questions and real-life examples have done so much to stimulate his thinking about Data Protection.

Special mention must also go to Stephen Lloyd of Bates Wells & Braithwaite for reading the book in draft and providing a welcome legal perspective. Any remaining errors and misunderstandings are, of course, the responsibility of the author alone.

Please note that this book does not set out to be a full statement of the law, and is not a substitute for professional legal advice on specific issues.

Second edition

This second edition includes new material based on experience with the Act since it came into force. In some areas, guidance from the Information Commissioner has become clearer. In others, problems have been addressed by practitioners and a consensus has started to emerge. Additional case studies and illustrative examples have been used to clarify many points, with several new flow charts to guide the reader through particularly tricky areas.

At the same time, the opportunity has been taken to make minor amendments in the light of legal and other changes.

About the author

Paul Ticher is a consultant and trainer working with national and local voluntary organisations. He specialises in information technology and good practice in information management, with a particular interest in Data Protection. Much of his work experience has been in the advice and information field, including five years as IT Adviser at the Community Information project (now absorbed into London Advice Services Alliance), where he undertook a considerable amount of work on the application of the 1984 Data Protection Act to voluntary organisations when it was first introduced. He has also worked in campaigning organisations and as Chief Officer of a small national charity.

Since the first edition of this book appeared, Paul has been a leading trainer on Data Protection throughout Britain, and he has advised many voluntary organisations on the subject.

e-mail: paul@paulticher.com

Definitions and abbreviations

Terms used in this book are defined briefly below and explained in more detail on the pages indicated.

The Act – the 1998 Data Protection Act.

Computer – used as a shorthand term in several places in this book. The Act refers to 'equipment operating automatically in response to instructions given for that purpose'.

Data – information held on computer or, in many cases, on paper, including photographs, video material etc., *see page 5*. In this book 'data' is treated as singular, like information, since this is becoming the accepted practice. Quotations directly from the Information Commissioner have 'data' used in the plural, and this has not been changed.

Data capture – the process of obtaining information from the **Data Subject**, either on paper forms or verbally, often used in the context of the **Data Controller**'s first contact with that person.

Data Controller – the organisation (or, occasionally, individual) responsible for how and why personal data is used, *see page 12*.

Data Processor – an organisation (or, occasionally, individual) to whom data processing has been outsourced, *see page 16*.

Data Protection Commissioner – the original name of the official responsible for enforcing Data Protection law under the 1998 Act, known as the Data Protection Registrar before 1 March 2000, now the Information Commissioner.

Data Protection Registrar – *see Data Protection Commissioner above.*

Data User – the 1984 Act equivalent of a **Data Controller**, *see page 12*.

Data Subject – an individual about whom personal data is held, *see page 9*.

Direct Marketing – 'the communication (by whatever means) of any advertising or marketing material which is directed to particular individuals', *see page 49*.

EU Directive 95/46/EC – the Directive, approved by the European Union on 24 October 1995, under which all member states had to bring in similar Data Protection legislation within three years. Limited areas were left to national discretion, but the main provisions apply throughout the European Union.

EU Directive 97/66/EC – the Directive under which marketing by telephone and fax is regulated, *see page 54*.

Information Commissioner – the official responsible for enforcing Data Protection and associated law. At the time of writing, the Commissioner was

Elizabeth France. In this book the Commissioner is therefore referred to as 'she'. However, Richard Thomas was due to take over the post in November 2002.

Manual records – used in this book (unless the context requires otherwise) to mean personal data held in a 'relevant filing system', *see page 6*.

Notification – the name under the 1998 Act for the equivalent to Registration under the 1984 Act. Some, but not all, Data Controllers have to 'notify' the Information Commissioner about the broad outline of their data processing activities.

Processing – any use of personal data, including obtaining, storing, using, disclosing or destroying it, *see page 27*.

Record – used in this book to mean a set of information about one individual.

Relevant filing system – manual (paper) files subject to the Data Protection Act, *see page 6*.

Sensitive personal data – special categories of data which have to be treated with special care, *see page 32*.

Introduction

Data Protection

Data Protection is a somewhat contradictory subject – it can come over as terribly dry and procedural, but it goes to the heart of very real individual concerns, with potentially serious impact on people's lives. If your GP transfers your records to computer and the old paper files end up in a skip for anyone to see, that's a Data Protection issue. If your bank confuses you with someone else and your credit rating plummets, that's also a Data Protection issue.

For voluntary organisations, building a relationship of trust with clients, volunteers and donors is not just desirable, but essential. Good Data Protection practice is an important part of this equation.

The UK has had Data Protection legislation since 1984, but the 1998 Data Protection Act saw a new departure: a Data Protection regime which offered genuine new rights to Data Subjects as well as providing a framework for responsible behaviour by those using personal data. The new regime was not implemented until nearly ten years after its initiation within the European Union. However, there was considerable consultation at various stages along the way, and the resulting legislation, while it could never be 'perfect', is workable and reasonable.

Voluntary organisations have no reason to fear the 1998 Act. In many ways it brings the law into line with good practices which have been developed and promoted in the sector ever since the 1984 Act. Compliance with the bureaucratic requirements is now, if anything, easier. This leaves Data Protection Officers free to concentrate on ensuring that their organisations have policies and procedures which genuinely protect the interests of Data Subjects.

At the heart of the Act is the concept of 'fairness'. If you handle information about people you have an overriding obligation to be fair. Fairness requires, in particular, 'transparency' – being open and honest with the Data Subject on how you are using information about them. It also means using their data in predictable ways, looking after the data and taking care that it doesn't get into the wrong hands. And who could argue with that? It's no more than we would expect from anyone who holds data about us.

Organisations which use data about individuals are faced with three options.

- Most voluntary organisations will be keen to follow best practice. This is not necessarily any more expensive than making the effort to find technical loopholes. It is the approach favoured in this book.
- Grudging compliance is an option for those wishing to circumvent the spirit of the new Act. As with any law, there are grey areas and special cases which can be exploited to avoid giving people the maximum benefit from the law.

- Ignoring the legislation has apparently been possible up to now for many of those who should have complied with the 1984 Act, but is obviously not recommended. Increasingly, it will not be an option as Data Subjects come to expect, and insist on, greater transparency and higher standards of compliance.

While good practice will not be very far from what many voluntary organisations are doing already, there are compliance issues to be aware of. There are even a very few circumstances in which Data Protection considerations may conflict with other concerns. (These are discussed at the appropriate points in the book.)

This book does not strictly follow the structure of the Act. Instead, it takes the reader step by step through the decision-making process in what is hoped is the most logical way. References to the text of the Act are made when appropriate, but the Act is not quoted in full.

It is important to be aware that the 1998 Data Protection Act has not been in force for long, and much of it has therefore not been tested in the courts. This means that its interpretation is often more of an art than a science. Much of our current understanding of the Act is based on guidance from the Information Commissioner. While authoritative, this is not legally binding. It is quite possible that the guidance might change, or be overturned by legal decisions. Day-to-day experience with the new Act will also contribute significantly to ideas on how best to put it into practice.

Readers are invited to contact the author with comments, or to seek further help on issues which are not adequately covered here.

Structure of the book

The 1998 Data Protection Act (generally referred to as 'the Act' in this book) sets out to provide a framework for the use of data about people. It aims to be fair to the individuals concerned without unduly hampering the person or organisation using the data, provided that their activities are reasonable.

All words and phrases in **bold** in this section are defined and discussed in more detail in later chapters. (See also page viii for an index of definitions and abbreviations.)

This book starts with an overview of the steps that most organisations are likely to have to take to bring themselves into compliance. It then looks at the Act in more detail.

The Act applies to **personal data**; that is, information about identifiable, living individuals which is held on computer or in many manual filing systems. The organisations or individuals which decide why and how personal data is **processed** (used in any way) are **Data Controllers**.

Chapter 2 looks in more detail at the definition of personal data, while Chapter 3 is concerned with identifying the Data Controller, in both straightforward and more complicated cases.

All Data Controllers have to follow the eight **Data Protection Principles**, a set of basic rules. These cover issues such as how to ensure fairness, the responsibility of the Data Controller to have good-quality data, and the Data Controller's security obligations. Chapter 4 looks briefly at all of the Principles.

Chapters 5 and 6 examine the issues surrounding 'fair' processing, particularly in relation to **sensitive data** – information about the Data Subject's racial or ethnic origin, beliefs, politics, health, sex life and criminal record. There are restrictions on using sensitive data, especially without the consent of the Data Subject.

In many situations getting the **consent** of the Data Subject is either necessary or advisable, but 'consent' is quite a tricky subject. When you might need it, and how you might get it, are discussed in Chapter 7.

Chapter 8 considers retention periods for data and looks at the circumstances when the Act affects archive material.

Among the new rights that the Act gives to Data Subjects is an absolute right to stop the Data Controller using their data for **direct marketing** – including charity fundraising and other common activities of voluntary organisations. This is examined in Chapter 9.

One of the principal requirements for fairness is that the Data Controller must ensure that the **Data Subject** knows who is processing data about them and what for. There are particular requirements to provide information when sensitive data is being processed, when data might be used for direct marketing, and when it might be passed on to other organisations or people. Chapter 10 summarises these considerations and looks at the kind of information the Data Controller ought to be providing to the Data Subject in various circumstances, and how it might be provided.

Chapter 11 summarises the main rights that a Data Subject has under the Act, while Chapter 12 examines one of the most important of these: the right of **Subject Access**, allowing people to see the data that is held about them.

Still with the Data Protection Principles, Chapter 13 considers the question of security, while Chapter 14 discusses the restrictions in the Act on transfer of data abroad.

Although the Act makes no specific reference to the Internet, e-mail data and information on the Web are covered by it. Chapter 15 pulls together a number of issues relating to the Internet, including reference to other relevant legislation.

Chapter 16 examines the Data Protection issues which might arise in the increasingly common situation where several organisations collaborate over service provision.

Many Data Controllers will have to **notify** the **Information Commissioner** about their Data Processing activities. This is covered in Chapter 17, while Chapter 18 looks at the enforcement powers of the Information Commissioner.

Chapters 19 and 20 review two specific areas of action – drawing up policies following an audit and ensuring that staff know how to comply with the Act on a day-to-day basis.

Background

The United Kingdom got its first Data Protection law – fittingly, as it seemed at the time – in 1984, the year of George Orwell's Big Brother. The law was introduced in order to allow the government to ratify a Data Protection Convention that had been drawn up by the Council of Europe. The limitations of the 1984 Act quickly became apparent. For organisations using data about people it imposed bureaucratic burdens, while offering very little benefit to individuals concerned about how their data was being used.

Very early in the life of the 1984 Act, criticisms began to emerge. At its heart it did very little to promote good practice in the use and management of personal data. Although it was based on fairly sound Data Protection principles, it allowed a Data User[1] to do more or less anything they wanted, provided that it was legal and that they had registered with the Data Protection Registrar in very broad terms what they intended to do.

The information a Data User had to provide when registering was so general and unspecific that it gave very little information to anyone seriously interested in finding out anything about a Data Processing operation. At the same time, filling in the forms was confusing and frustrating, and – particularly for small voluntary organisations – the registration fee was a significant disincentive. Hardly surprisingly, only an estimated 40% of those legally required to register actually did so.

A Data Subject wanting to check up on the data held about them could be faced with paying one organisation several, or in some cases even dozens, of £10 fees in order to cover all the possibilities. It is said that to see all the information held on one person by the Metropolitan Police could have cost £350.

---

[1] Under the 1984 Act a Data User was any organisation or person who 'holds or controls' personal data. The 1998 Act equivalent is a Data Controller.

On top of all this, the enforcement powers of the Data Protection Registrar were limited. Despite the heroic efforts at persuasion by successive Registrars, and their judicious use of the legal powers available, Data Protection under the 1984 Act never had much real day-to-day impact.

The limitations of the 1984 Act were widely acknowledged within a short time, and pressure grew for the most obvious problems, at least, to be ameliorated. However, the Home Office took the view that it did not want to legislate again in this area too quickly. Quite soon, the European Union began debating harmonisation of its Data Protection laws, and this was then given as a valid reason for making no change in the UK, only to have to make another set of changes once the European position was finalised.

Unfortunately, while the debate in Europe dragged on well into the 1990s, the Home Office steadfastly stood by its decision to wait. Even the most obvious changes could not be made without recourse to Parliament because the very fine detail of the 1984 Act was enshrined in the primary legislation itself. Successive Data Protection Registrars did the best they could – for example to simplify the registration process – but had very limited room for manoeuvre.

Eventually on 24 October 1995 the European Union agreed Directive 95/46/EC on the harmonisation of Data Protection laws. This gave member states three years to enact domestic legislation to put the Directive into effect. The UK government was still unenthusiastic about Europe, and dragged its feet – even for a while considering minor amendments to the 1984 Act rather than the wholesale revision that was merited.

For some, this turned out to be a blessing in disguise, as it gave a clean start to the new government which took office in May 1997. Commendably quickly, in August 1997, there appeared a White Paper, committing the government to implementing the spirit as well as the letter of the European Directive. This was followed, after a short period of consultation, by a Bill which had its first reading in January 1998.

Instead of incorporating all the detail into the Bill, as had been done in 1984, the 1998 legislation laid down a broad structure, leaving much of the detail to be completed through secondary legislation. This has the important advantage that if changes have to be made in future, they can be brought in much more easily, without the need for a new law. We should no longer have to live with unworkable provisions, merely because the effort of changing them is judged to be not worth it.

However, an unfortunate consequence was that Royal Assent for the new law on 16 July 1998 was not the end of the story. The law could not take effect until some thirty pieces of secondary legislation had been prepared, consulted on, and brought before Parliament. Despite the deadline set in the European Directive, the UK – in common with most other EU member states – started to fall behind schedule. In fact it was 1 March 2000 before the Act finally came into effect. Another step closer to the final stage was made on 24 October 2001, when the main transitional period ended and the new regime came fully into force.

Has all the effort been worth it? There is no doubt that the new legislation does overcome many of the most obvious flaws in the old Act.

- Data Subjects are given real, if limited, controls over how their information is used.
- There is provision for much greater transparency: Data Subjects should know much more from now on about who is doing what with information about them.
- The impenetrable and unhelpful format for registration has been replaced with a slightly simpler system of notification.
- Above all, the Act now incorporates much good practice. In the past, complying with the Act and following good practice, while by no means mutually exclusive, were almost two separate exercises.

The new Act requires all those who use personal data – not just those who hold it on computer and not just those who have to notify – to be fair and responsible in the way they use it.

Whatever flaws and problems emerge over the coming years, the 1998 Act is a much better starting point for all concerned – both those who use data about people, and the people whose data is being used.

The task ahead

Data Protection compliance is not usually about following a set of discrete rules. Your activities *as a whole* have to produce the right result, and you have to take a broad view over all your areas of work to ensure that this is the case.

This chapter:

▶ Summarises the steps you need to take in order to comply with the Data Protection Act

Before plunging into the detail of the 1998 Data Protection Act and what it means, it might be useful to consider some of the main themes.

Instinctively, most voluntary organisations would comply with perhaps 90% of the Data Protection Act, even in the absence of legislation. This is because voluntary organisations believe in, and often actually exist to promote, individual rights. Strict client confidentiality is already a central concern for most voluntary organisations, and the vast majority have no interest in exploiting or upsetting their staff, their donors, their volunteers or their other contacts.

The first message is therefore not to panic or worry unduly. In many voluntary organisations existing practice will not have to be changed much to bring it into line with the legal requirements in the Act. In practice, you can achieve compliance in many areas by common sense and a basic respect for the Data Subject.

Having decided to tackle Data Protection, you will have to work in three broad areas:

- clarifying responsibilities and specific legal obligations;
- carrying out an audit and then making a risk assessment to ensure that you prioritise action in the areas where it is most needed;
- training or briefing *all* your paid staff and volunteers who have contact with personal data to understand their responsibilities.

In terms of responsibilities and legal compliance, you need to do the following:

- Identify the Data Controller, or Controllers, in respect of all the personal data you handle (see Chapters 2 and 16). Normally your organisation will be the Data Controller. Where you have a complex organisational structure, or work closely with other organisations, things may not be so straightforward.
- Ensure that your board or management committee is aware of its responsibilities for Data Protection compliance and makes the necessary decisions.
- Allocate a senior member of staff to have an overview of Data Protection within your organisation, and possibly give additional responsibilities to department heads or team leaders.
- Put in place procedures for handling any Subject Access requests (see Chapter 12).
- Review your employment contracts and volunteer agreements to ensure that Data Protection responsibilities are adequately covered.
- Review your contractual arrangements with any Data Processor you outsource work to (see Chapter 3).
- Ensure that your notification is accurate and up to date (see Chapter 17). This can only really be done after you have carried out your audit.

The style of audit recommended by the Information Commissioner can be lengthy, detailed and time consuming. You may eventually decide that this is appropriate for you. Initially, however, you need to get an idea of what is most urgent, by identifying your main likely problem areas. Suggestions for how to do this can be found in Chapter 19.

This process may well throw up questions that need to be resolved. You may need advice from your umbrella body or from an external professional, or you may need to make decisions – for example whether to seek consent from certain Data Subjects in order to comply with the Fair Processing Conditions.

Before training your staff and volunteers it is worth having a written policy (see Chapter 19). This should not be a lengthy document, but should clarify the standards that you wish to meet and any specific procedures designed to achieve this. For example, you may want everyone to use a consistent phrasing when they offer people a marketing opt-out. The policy should also spell out any specific decisions you have made – for example on whether you will charge for Subject Access and who will handle Subject Access requests to your organisation.

Short training sessions, repeated for new staff, and with refreshers once or twice a year, are better than long detailed sessions that are never followed up. Often these sessions are best carried out at the team level, where people can discuss case studies that are particularly relevant to their work.

In all this, your main concerns should be on:

- **Transparency** – making sure that your Data Subjects are not kept in the dark about what you are doing, especially about non-obvious uses of their data or conditions under which you would disclose their data to other people.
- **Data Subject rights** – in particular the right to opt out of direct marketing, which includes fundraising and other unsolicited contacts.
- **Reliable, consistent systems and procedures** – so that when a Data Subject gives consent, expresses a preference or tells you that their data has changed, this is recorded accurately right across the organisation.
- **Security** – being confident that all your trustees or committee members, staff and volunteers will maintain confidentiality and ensure that data is not used inappropriately.

The following chapters explain the Act in more detail.

What is personal data?

Whatever information you hold about people, most of it will be subject to the terms of the Data Protection Act. But in some instances – largely arising when the information is held on paper but not in a filing system – the Act does not apply. The easiest option may be to assume that, for most purposes, *all* personal information is covered. That way, you can't go wrong. You may, however, feel you need to know more about the scope of the Act to decide on the best course of action for your organisation.

This chapter explains:

▶ How to decide which types of information are covered by the Data Protection Act and which are not

The 1998 Data Protection Act is concerned with 'personal data'. In order to be covered by the Act, information must be personal *and* it must be data, as defined by the Act (see box defining 'data' on page 5). The 'personal' part is relatively straightforward, referring to data about:

- identifiable ▪ living ▪ individuals.

It therefore does not apply to information about companies or organisations, but it could apply to named contacts within those organisations. It does not apply to data which is completely anonymous, but it does apply if you can identify the people from the data combined with other information you hold. It does not apply (except in a very few situations) to information about people who have died, and it does not apply to fictitious people.

When the Act says that people must be 'identifiable' this does not mean simply that the data must include their name. They are identifiable if you have any way of working out who they are from information you possess or might reasonably be expected to possess. You might number your case files, but if you have a list that matches the numbers to clients' names, then the case files are identifiable – even if access to the list is restricted. Even without a name someone might be identifiable: the single parent with three children living in a particular street could be obvious to many people in the community; someone in a photograph might be identifiable from distinctive clothing or other attributes.

> ### I have a database of organisations. Surely names of my contact people don't count?
>
> Actually, they do. You probably know their name, their employer, their job title or position, their direct phone line, their e-mail address ... However, the consequences of this being personal data are usually minimal, provided you use the information in obvious business-related ways. You do have to be more careful with very small voluntary organisations: the contact details they gave you may be someone's home address and phone number.

'Data' is a much trickier concept. It is defined in the Act under four headings and a fifth was added in the Freedom of Information Act 2000, although this was not in force at the time of writing. The full definition is given in the box, but for most voluntary organisations data essentially amounts to:

- information held on computer;
- information in 'relevant' manual files;
- information intended to become part of one of the above systems.

Data[2]

means information which:

(a) is being processed by means of equipment operating automatically in response to instructions given for that purpose,

(b) is recorded with the intention that it should be processed by means of such equipment,

(c) is recorded as part of a relevant filing system or with the intention that it should form part of a relevant filing system,

(d) does not fall within paragraph (a), (b) or (c) but forms part of an accessible record as defined by section 68, or the Freedom of Information Act 2000, or

(e) is recorded information held by a public authority and does not fall within any of paragraphs (a) to (d).[3]

Categories (d) and (e) relate to bodies legally defined as carrying out public functions only – see Chapter 16.

The definition of data is wide, and the 1998 Act extends the definition in the 1984 Act in four main ways.

---

[2] See paragraph 1 of the Act for all definitions quoted in this chapter and the next.
[3] Added through the Freedom of Information Act 2000, s. 68(2) and expected to come into force in January 2005.

- The 1984 Act excluded certain information held on computer; the 1998 Act makes no exceptions.
- The 1984 Act did not cover paper systems; the 1998 Act does.
- The 1998 Act introduces a new category covering material intended to be put onto computer or to become part of a relevant manual system.
- The 1998 Act much more explicitly covers non-text data such as photographs, audio and video material, and biometric data (such as fingerprints, iris patterns or DNA samples).

'Computer' is used above as shorthand for any equipment operating automatically.

It is particularly important to note that 'data' does not just mean text. Photographs and video recordings, in particular, must now be treated much more carefully if they relate to identifiable, living people. See Appendix D for a discussion of the range of issues that might arise with photographs and videos.

You should also think about personal data in less obvious places: the phone numbers stored in your mobile phone, the log that records access to a building protected by a swipe-card entry system, or client details transferred to your diary in preparation for a series of home visits.

Just because these might be personal data, it doesn't necessarily follow that you are doing anything wrong at the moment. But, to be sure, you do need to review your practice.

Surely Data Protection doesn't apply to information that is already in the public domain, like the names of chief officers of voluntary organisations or our local councillors?

Yes it does. There may be very little restriction on using the information, but you still have to be 'fair' to the Data Subject, as discussed in Chapter 5.

What is a 'relevant filing system'?

Ever since the 1995 EU Directive came out there has been debate over which manual records are covered, and this was the subject of considerable discussion in Parliament.

The Directive states that it should apply to manual systems only 'if the data processed are contained or are intended to be contained in a filing system structured according to specific criteria relating to individuals, so as to permit easy access to the personal data in question'.

It then goes on to define a 'personal data filing system' as 'any structured set of personal data which are accessible according to specific criteria, whether centralised, decentralised or dispersed on a functional or geographical basis'.

The definition which the UK government came up with, and the one which is in the Act (after minor amendment in Parliament) was significantly different.

Relevant filing system

means any set of information [not on a computer] relating to individuals to the extent that… the set is structured, either by reference to individuals or by reference to criteria relating to individuals, in such a way that specific information relating to a particular individual is readily accessible.

The government has clearly attempted to narrow the definition down by inserting the condition that 'specific information relating to a particular individual' must be readily accessible. In Parliament it was stated that only very limited sets of highly structured data should be caught. However, the Information Commissioner expressed public disagreement with the government's interpretation, and set out a far wider definition than the government would like.[4]

It is probably safest to take a fairly broad view, and to treat borderline cases on the assumption that they are covered. This means that any file or set of files (or, for example, a box of index cards) where you can go easily to the information about a specific individual is quite likely to be within the Act.

Examples of material which is probably *not* personal data include the minutes of meetings. Even if confidential personal matters are discussed, the material isn't generally organised so that you can 'readily' find 'specific information'.

Be wary, however, of assuming that manually-held data is outside the Act. Even if the file itself is disorganised, the more easily you can look up information about specific individuals, the more likely it is to be personal data. For instance, if you put the booking forms for your training courses into files by course, but have a separate record of who has attended each one, the forms in the files are likely to be personal data.

Note that the information must be in a 'set'. A single phone number on a sticky note wouldn't be covered, but an alphabetical list of personal phone numbers might be.

This is such a complex area that anomalies are bound to be thrown up. Once the Act has been in place for some time, guidance from the Information Commissioner, and even case law, will begin to clarify some of the issues.

---

[4] It is also possible for the Directive itself to over-ride UK law if it can be shown that the UK government has not accurately implemented the Directive.

Is it personal data?

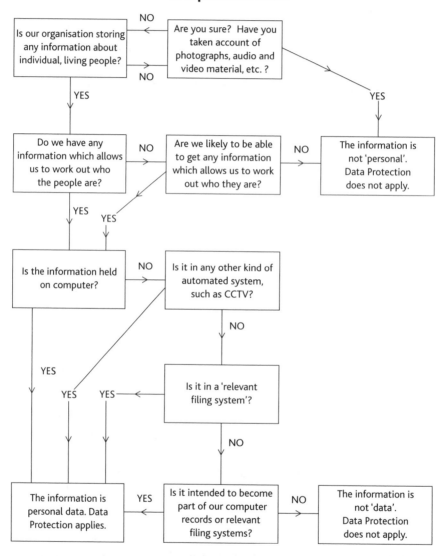

Information intended to go onto computer or into the files

There are potentially important consequences from the inclusion as data of material intended to form part of a computer or manual record. What this means is that the 'data capture' documents on which you collect information come within the scope of the Act, even if you discard them as soon as the data is in your system. Application forms, booking forms and interview notes are just some examples of what could be covered by this element of the Act.

All the responsibilities of Data Controllers – to act fairly, to ensure appropriate security, and not to keep data longer than necessary, for example (as discussed below) – apply with equal force to these 'data capture' documents.

The Data Subject

A Data Subject is anyone whose personal data is processed. While you may be able to identify most of your 'primary' Data Subjects without difficulty, it is worth paying attention to the inadvertent creation of 'secondary' Data Subjects. For example, if you have a personnel system, your staff will clearly be Data Subjects. However, you may well ask them for details of next of kin, or emergency contacts. If these details are put on computer, the additional people are also likely to be Data Subjects, with all the rights that this involves (as described in later chapters).

If your personnel records are in manual files the emergency contacts may not be Data Subjects because you can't 'readily' find out anything about them; you can only go by the staff member's name on the file. However, if you routinely collect information about the partners and children of staff members, there may be a case for claiming that these people could be readily located, even in manual files.

> **I only have information about people overseas. Are they Data Subjects?**
>
> Yes. There is no geographical restriction.

Data Subjects can also be people who have provided information about someone else. A social worker, for example, or someone who provides a reference, may be a Data Subject if their name goes onto your computer. Even if it doesn't, they generally have specific rights if the person they have provided information about wants to see their file (see Chapter 12).

Summary

Most information that voluntary organisations hold about people will be 'personal data', and therefore covered by the Act.

In the vast majority of cases there will be no dispute. Examples include:

- client or case records;
- records of staff and volunteers;
- membership records;
- newsletter mailing lists;
- fundraising or supporter databases;
- training administration records (whether for external or internal courses);
- most conference administration and bookings systems;
- contact databases (unless they contain information exclusively about organisations, with no named individuals);
- computer-based sales records, where the purchaser's details are kept;
- lists of consultants, trainers or other resource people.

The two key questions are: is it 'personal', and is it 'data'? If the answer to both is 'yes', then the set of information is covered by the Act.

When identifying Data Subjects, you must take into account *all* the people you have information about, not just your primary Data Subjects.

EXAMPLES

① Maria runs a befriending service which uses a couple of dozen volunteers. When anyone applies to be a volunteer they fill in a form, which then gets filed. There is a separate file for each volunteer, and they are in alphabetical order. Holiday records and training records are also kept in these files. Should Maria treat the files as personal data?

She quickly realises that in this manual system she can easily find specific information about particular people, and therefore that it should be treated as personal data.

② Martin has a complaints file where complaints are received from individuals. Much of the content is highly sensitive, so he might expect Data Protection rules to apply automatically.

However, the file is merely in date order, according to when each complaint was received, with no index. Martin concludes that it probably does not fall within the definition of data. He cannot go to the file with the intention of finding information about a specific, known individual.

On the other hand, were he to go and reorganise it so that the complaints are filed in alphabetical order of the person who complained, then the likelihood is that it would be covered.

There is even a third possibility: if all the complaints about each member of staff were filed together, then the set of information might be personal data about the staff members rather than about the complainants.

③ Rajan is surprised to see a Data Protection statement in the reception area of a big multi-national company which is hosting a conference for his organisation. They use closed-circuit television (CCTV)[5] to monitor each area of the office for security purposes and their security manager has decided that the contents of the tapes may well be personal data. To be safe, the company publicises this prominently.

④ A telephone helpline takes a lot of details about its callers, but allows them to remain anonymous. Susan, the operations manager, transfers the information to computer so that she can analyse the pattern of calls. Is the information on computer personal data? What about the paper records of calls?

Susan realises that if all the information on the computer is anonymous and there is no way of identifying the people via other information (on paper, for example), then the computer database is not personal data. The paper records might be personal data if they include the names of people who rang up and they are filed so that individual people's records can be easily found, in which case the computer record would be personal data too.

⑤ William is a personnel manager in a large charity. He gets a lot of people writing in asking about employment. They are each sent a personalised, word-processed letter, and their enquiry is put in a big file called 'Employment Enquiries'. When a vacancy comes up, someone looks through the file and sends the details of the job to anyone who looks suitable. William wonders whether the 'employment enquiries' file might be personal data? And what about the word-processed reply letters?

Eventually William decides that the 'employment enquiries' file is not personal data. Technically, he thinks that the word-processed letters could be personal data, even if the personalised letter is not saved. (In practice, however, he realises that the consequences of the letters being personal data are likely to be minimal.)

---

[5] CCTV was the subject of one of the first Codes of Practice issued by the Information Commissioner under the 1998 Act. The Code is available on the Commissioner's website.

3

Who is the Data Controller?

Legal responsibility for compliance with the Act lies with the Data Controller. Normally this will be an organisation, not individual staff or volunteers. If you outsource any activities which involve the use of (or access to) personal data, you are dealing with a Data Processor.

This chapter looks at:

▶ How to identify the Data Controller, particularly in more complex situations where this may not be straightforward

▶ The relationship between the Data Processor and your organisation

The concept of the Data Controller is an important element in the 1998 Act. If you are a Data Controller, the Act applies to you. If you are not a Data Controller, your responsibilities are more limited. You need to work out, therefore, whether you are a Data Controller (or, more likely, whether your organisation is a Data Controller).

The definition appears, at first sight, quite straightforward. The Data Controller is whoever decides why and how personal data is to be processed.

> **Data Controller**
>
> means ... a person who (either alone or jointly or in common with other persons) determines the purposes for which and the manner in which any personal data are, or are to be, processed;

The first point to note is that the definition uses the word 'person', not 'individual'. In other words, a legal 'person' – such as a limited company – can be a Data Controller. An 'unincorporated' organisation is not a legal person,[6] which would appear to mean that such an organisation cannot then be the Data Controller.

However, the practice under the 1984 Act was to allow unincorporated associations to register in the name of the organisation, rather than under its

---

[6] Don't forget that whether your organisation is incorporated or not has nothing to do with whether it is a charity or not. It could be both incorporated and a charity, or one and not the other, or neither. See Appendix A for a note on this issue.

trustees. The Information Commissioner has indicated that this approach is to continue, with the Commissioner happy to treat the organisation itself as the Data Controller. Whether this will be the final position remains to be seen. The view favoured by many lawyers is that each individual on the Management Committee or Board of Trustees may technically be a Data Controller, acting 'jointly' with the others.

For most day-to-day purposes you can probably behave as though an unincorporated organisation is in fact the Data Controller. However, it is as well that your Committee or Trustees are made aware of the precise situation. If in any doubt about what this means, you should take qualified legal advice.

Joint activities and consortia

There are likely to be situations where two organisations, acting jointly or in common, are Data Controllers of the same personal data.

As a general guide, the likely situation is that if two or more organisations are using the same data for the same purpose(s) they will be 'joint' Data Controllers. Either could be liable to pay compensation for any breaches of Data Protection, even if the mistake was actually made by the other Data Controller. If they are pooling data to use for different purposes – for example where they each have separate data about the Data Subject that only the originating organisation can see and use – they will be acting 'in common', liable only for their own actions. For example, you may be organising a conference in collaboration with another organisation, deciding together on the 'purposes' for which the personal data is collected and the 'manner' in which it is processed. Both organisations will share the responsibility as joint Data Controllers.

It is increasingly common for several organisations to get together in a formal consortium and agree to share client data, so that a person known to one organisation in the consortium does not have to provide their details all over again when they approach another. If they share just the basic contact details, but then add their own specific case records, it is likely that the organisations would each be Data Controllers, acting in common – but they could end up carrying some of the responsibility if another member of the consortium breached the Act. The implications of collaborative work are explored in Chapter 16.

> **Our parent body has told us that they will cover us for Data Protection. Is this OK?**
>
> Probably not. You cannot *choose* to be a Data Controller on someone else's behalf. The question is, 'Where are the decisions made?' If you are given strict instructions by your parent body, and have no leeway, then they could well be the Data Controller. However, if the local organisation is independent enough to make its own decisions and set up its own systems it is more likely to be a Data Controller in its own right.

When might an individual be a Data Controller?

An individual employee is never likely to be the Data Controller of personal data which is used by an organisation in the course of its activities. The Data Controller will be either the organisation itself or the trustees or committee members who carry the final responsibility. The staff member will merely be an 'agent' of the Data Controller.

However, the case may be less clear when it comes to volunteers or to self-employed people who carry out a particular service for the organisation. Although it is clear that an employee is most unlikely to be a Data Controller, members of the Information Commissioner's staff have indicated that they believe this applies to volunteers as well. Employees, volunteers and contract workers are all likely to be 'agents' of the Data Controller. You would, however, have to look carefully at who actually made the decisions and took responsibility for the data in order to decide who is the Data Controller.

Self-employed people may well be Data Controllers in their own right. Organisations should ensure that any transfer of data to freelance workers or other external contractors complies with the Data Protection Principles (see Chapter 4).

> **Does my private Christmas card list make me a Data Controller?**
>
> No. The Act does not apply to genuine domestic use. Someone using a home computer to maintain their Christmas card list is totally exempt. This exemption does not apply, however, if you handle personal data at home on behalf of an organisation, even a small, informal, voluntary one with no money and no staff. Even holding a card index recording the birthdays of children who attend your local playgroup could make you a Data Controller. (But the Data Controller would be the playgroup if it had asked you to do this.)

Am I a Data Controller, and if not, who is?

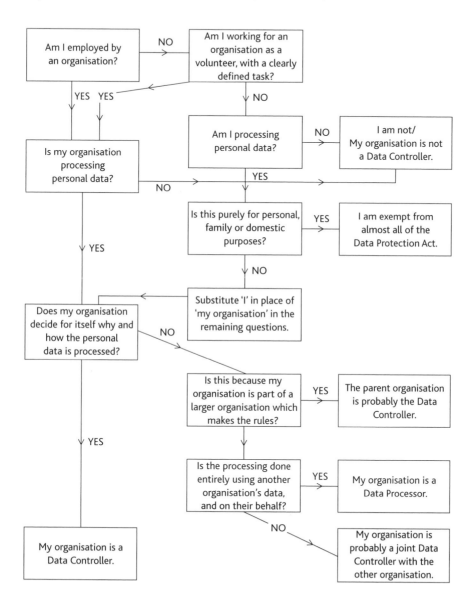

Where there is a serious possibility of confusion, it is likely to be worth establishing the situation very clearly on paper – possibly through your contract if you are paying people for services. Again, qualified legal advice is strongly recommended.

Even where individuals are clearly not Data Controllers, many organisations will wish to identify a specific staff member or member of the governing body as Data Protection Compliance Officer. This person will have a clear responsibility to be informed about Data Protection issues, to ensure that the organisation complies with its obligations, and to train or brief other staff in what they are allowed to do, what they are not allowed to do, and what to do if they are in any doubt. See also Chapter 20.

> ### I work with partner organisations abroad. Are they Data Controllers?
>
> The UK Act only applies to organisations that have a base, or process their data, in the UK. If your partners are independent, they will be subject to their own local Data Protection law, if any. If the relationship is not totally independent, it would be worth taking advice. See also Chapter 14.

Data Processors

Instead of, or even as well as, being a Data Controller, an organisation may be a Data Processor. This is defined in the Act.

> ### Data Processor
>
> … means any person (other than an employee[7] of the Data Controller) who processes the data on behalf of the Data Controller;

The Act goes on to lay down conditions applying to a Data Processor. The key points are as follows.

- The Data Processor must be following directions from the Data Controller. If they have any discretion at all, the chances are that the organisation is not a Data Processor but a Data Controller in its own right.
- There must be a written contract between the Data Controller and the Data Processor.
- The Data Processor has a specific duty to take adequate security measures (see Chapter 13).
- The Data Controller has a responsibility to satisfy itself that the Data Processor's security is appropriate.

---

[7] Here again, the Information Commissioner suggests that volunteers are 'agents' of the Data Controller, not Data Processors.

Note that an individual – such as a freelance worker or other contractor – can be a Data Processor, which is especially likely if they are providing a service to your organisation in return for money.

The important point is that the Data Controller remains responsible for what happens to the data, and liable for any mistakes. If you outsource your payroll, for example, your employees would still quite rightly complain to you if they didn't get paid. You, not the Data Processor, would have to compensate them if they incurred bank charges as a result. Your remedy would be to have provision in your contract with the Data Processor for them to reimburse you. Otherwise you would just have to accept your loss as the penalty for choosing a less than perfect supplier of payroll services.

In some cases where two organisations share data it may not be easy to distinguish between several possible relationships.

- They might be joint Data Controllers of a common set of data.
- One organisation might be the Data Controller, with another acting as a Data Processor.
- One organisation might be the Data Controller, making regular disclosures of information to the other. The recipient organisation may or may not be a Data Controller in its own right, depending on the form in which the data is disclosed and the way it is subsequently handled.

Summary

- Most organisations will be Data Controllers, or can behave as though they are.
- Individuals are unlikely to be Data Controllers in their role as employees or volunteers, although in other circumstances an individual can certainly be a Data Controller.
- An organisation should consider identifying a member of staff or the governing body as Data Protection Compliance Officer.
- Where two or more organisations share data closely, they need to be particularly careful to identify their respective Data Protection responsibilities clearly, and in many cases will find it best to state them in writing.

EXAMPLES

⑥ Harry and Sally are outreach workers from two different drugs organisations. They decide to organise a one-off conference for colleagues in the sector. Between them they work out: what information to collect on the booking form, whether to send people confirmation slips when they book, which details are included in the participants' list available at the conference, and so on. Because Sally has a better computer, they decide that she will actually set up and manage the database where the participants' details are kept.

They do not set up a separate organisation to run the conference, but they agree that both organisations are likely to be joint Data Controllers with respect to the data they collect. Luckily, both organisations have already included training and conference administration as a purpose in their notification to the Information Commissioner, and there is no need to update their notification entries.

Because Sally is running the database, they decide to base their Data Protection policy on her organisation's approach and, in particular, to adopt her security policy. Their materials, where relevant, have to identify both organisations as Data Controllers.

⑦ Brian is a keen member of his local church. Without consulting anyone, he plans to build up a small database on his home computer of people who are likely to help with the annual Christmas Fair. Just in time, he realises that this will make him a Data Controller. He decides it would be better if the church were the Data Controller, so hands over control before starting the project.

⑧ A mediation service uses self-employed sessional mediators. The case notes are recorded by the mediators and kept by them. The service knows which clients are on which mediators' case-list, but holds no further details. The service has strict rules on confidentiality but makes no other rules about what information should be recorded or how it should be kept. This raises the possibility of each individual mediator being the Data Controller for the information they hold (depending on how they hold it). After consultation, the organisation decides that it would be better to issue clear instructions to the mediators about what to hold and how, including rules on security and confidentiality, to make it clear that the organisation is the Data Controller.

⑨ Veronica is in charge of fundraising at a large charity. In addition to mailing their previous donors, they have a contract with a specialist telephone fundraising agency which calls people to ask for money. Because there is a written contract, and because this makes it clear that it is the charity which makes all the decisions, then the fundraising agency is a Data Processor, with the charity remaining the Data Controller at all times.

However, Veronica has also developed a small 'Friends of the Centenary Project' group of volunteers. She gives them the names and details of the 500 top donors and says, in effect, 'Raise as much money from these people as you can, in whatever way you think best.' Unless she makes this relationship more formal, she realises that in this case the group of volunteers would almost certainly be a Data Controller in its own right.

The Data Protection Principles

Everything you do with personal data has to comply with the eight Data Protection Principles contained in the Data Protection Act. Each Principle is explored in more detail in later chapters.

This chapter gives:

▶ An overview of the eight Data Protection Principles in the Act

At the heart of the 1998 Act is the list of eight Data Protection Principles. Although the 1984 Act also had eight Principles, many of which are similar, there are crucial differences. The most important change is that the Data Protection Principles now apply to *all* Data Controllers. Under the 1984 Act, they applied only to those who had to register. Even a Data Controller that only processes[8] manual data is now bound by the Principles.

Principle 1 concerns 'fair' processing, and sets out in some detail actions that Data Controllers must take, as well as conditions they must meet in order to avoid being unfair. Unfortunately, it cannot be fully understood without reference to Schedules 2 and 3 of the Act (Schedule 1 covers the Principles themselves). Unlike the Data Protection Principles in the 1984 Act, therefore, the new ones don't lend themselves so easily to being used for briefing staff on how to work within the Act. Some ideas on how to present the new Act to staff and volunteers are given in Chapter 20.

Principle 2 is less specific than its equivalent in the 1984 Act. Previously, the rule was simple because it was based on registration: you had to register what you were going to do and then you could only use data for the purpose(s) that you had registered.

Under the 1998 Act the Data Controller still has to have a 'specified' purpose or purposes, but they may not have to notify the Information Commissioner (the new equivalent of registration). This means that notification is now just one way in which you can specify a purpose. The other, if you are not required to notify, is to specify the purpose directly to the Data Subject.

---

[8]   See the full definition of 'processing' in the following chapter.

The Data Protection Principles[9]

1   Personal data shall be processed fairly and lawfully and, in particular, shall not be processed unless –
   (a) at least one of the conditions in Schedule 2[10] is met, and
   (b) in the case of sensitive personal data, at least one of the conditions in Schedule 3 is also met.
2   Personal data shall be obtained only for one or more specified and lawful purposes, and shall not be further processed in any manner incompatible with that purpose or those purposes.
3   Personal data shall be adequate, relevant and not excessive in relation to the purpose or purposes for which they are processed.
4   Personal data shall be accurate and, where necessary, kept up to date.
5   Personal data processed for any purpose or purposes shall not be kept for longer than is necessary for that purpose or those purposes.
6   Personal data shall be processed in accordance with the rights of data subjects under this Act.
7   Appropriate technical and organisational measures shall be taken against unauthorised or unlawful processing of personal data and against accidental loss or destruction of, or damage to, personal data.
8   Personal data shall not be transferred to a country or territory outside the European Economic Area unless that country or territory ensures an adequate level of protection for the rights and freedoms of data subjects in relation to the processing of personal data.

The 'purposes' defined for the 1998 Act are generally broader than those for the 1984 Act, and a single purpose can encompass a wide range of activities. Examples of purposes include:[11]

- **Staff administration**: appointments or removals, pay, discipline, superannuation, work management or other personnel matters in relation to the staff of the Data Controller.
- **Consultancy and advisory services**: giving advice or rendering professional services. The provision of services of an advisory, consultancy or intermediary nature. You will be asked to indicate the nature of the services which you provide.
- **Fundraising** in support of your objectives.
- **Processing for not-for-profit organisations**: establishing or maintaining membership of or support for a body or association which is not established or conducted for profit, or providing or administering activities for individuals who are either members of the body or association or have regular contact with it.

[9] Schedule 1, Part I of the Act.
[10] See the following chapter for more about Schedules 2 and 3.
[11] These are quoted from the Information Commissioner's *Notification Handbook: a complete guide to notification.*

- **Realising the objectives of a charitable organisation or voluntary body**: the provision of goods or services in order to realise the objectives of the charity or voluntary body.

Principle 2 also contains the important provision that all your processing must be compatible with the purpose(s) you obtained the data for. This means that you cannot, for example, disclose information to someone else unless you are sure that the disclosure is compatible. Even within your organisation, if your service is confidential you must restrict access on a 'need to know' basis. A management committee member leafing through the client files, just because they felt like it, would probably breach the second Principle.

Principles 3, 4 and 5 are very similar to their equivalents in the 1984 Act, and essentially insist that data should be of good quality. While there may be specific cases in which it is hard to draw a clear line, most Data Controllers would in any case want to follow these principles.

Note that it is up to the Data Controller in the first instance to decide what is 'necessary', although there may be legal considerations, especially about how long it is necessary to keep personal data.

In Principles 3 and 5 the decision on whether the data meets the criteria must be taken in relation to the purpose(s) for which it is being processed.

Principle 6 covers Data Subject rights. These include the right of access to their data, now including manual files, and the right to prevent processing in certain cases – in particular where direct marketing is concerned. (For more details on this, see Chapter 9.)

Principle 7 imposes a duty to have appropriate security, again now applying to manual as well as computerised records. You may have to restrict access to files by staff or volunteers, unless they have a good reason, as well as people outside the organisation.

'Organisational' security measures could include drawing up policies and procedures and training staff to follow them. 'Technical' measures include physical access control, such as locks on doors and filing cabinets, as well as things like computer passwords and back-up procedures.

When a Data Controller 'notifies', they will have to provide certain information about their security measures.

The question of security is addressed further in Chapter 13.

Principle 8 caused considerable disagreement between the European Union and the USA. The US government specifically rejected the idea of Data Protection legislation, and it appeared at one point as though data transfer between the European Union and the USA (as well as most other countries) would be seriously hampered by this principle. The commercial ramifications would have been inestimable, and a political solution was required. See Chapter 14 for more details.

Summary

- All 'processing' of personal data must be 'fair'.
- You must collect and use personal data only for specified purposes.
- The data must be adequate, relevant and not excessive.
- The data must be accurate and up to date.
- The data must not be held longer than necessary.
- Data Subjects' rights must be respected.
- You must have appropriate security.
- Special rules apply to transfers of personal data abroad.

EXAMPLES

⑩ Nirmal's advice agency receives most of its funding from the local council, under a contract. One year, the council announces that it is changing the conditions of its contract. In order to ensure that the funds are spent only on eligible clients, it wants to inspect random case records as part of its monitoring procedure.

Nirmal and his colleagues are understandably upset at the thought that the council officers may be seeing their confidential records, and worry about the effect this might have on clients. They wonder if they can refuse on Data Protection grounds.

One issue here is whether disclosing the records to the council officers (which is certainly 'processing') is compatible with the purpose(s) for which the data was originally collected. Would the agency be breaking the second Data Protection Principle?

Nirmal looks into it and decides provisionally that the agency has a case for refusing access. If the monitoring were for quality control, it would be possible to argue that this was an integral part of providing the service, and it therefore would be compatible with the original purpose. But auditing the agency's use of funds is a separate activity. The agency therefore asks the council to reconsider, and to look for a way of monitoring that does not involve breaches of either client confidentiality or Data Protection.

⑪ Melissa runs an organisation that promotes good childcare. Over time, it has built up a database of many of the local childminders, which it uses to send out relevant information and invitations to training events. The organisation gets a lot of phone calls from people asking if they can recommend a childminder in the area, but the organisation is reluctant to do this. Instead, it considers publishing its database as a list which people could use to make their own selection.

However, Melissa points out that in her view this is a completely different purpose from the original one of providing direct services to the childminders. If the organisation wants to do this, she feels that it needs to go back to the people on the database and, in effect, collect the data anew for this new purpose.

⑫ A community transport organisation starts to get comments from its drivers that they need to have more information about the service users in order to provide a good service. If they knew that someone needed help getting from their door to the vehicle, for example, the drivers could get out straight away and offer the help. They argue that it is relevant to providing the service, and therefore compatible with the third Data Protection Principle. The Management Committee agrees and decides to collect this additional information from service users who are happy to give it.

The committee also decides that they need to be careful not to collect too much data. They don't actually need to know the person's specific disability, just the kind of support that they might need. So they redesign their record forms to ask very direct questions: 'Do you want the driver to come to your door to assist?' 'Can you get into the vehicle without the hoist?' 'Will you normally have a dog with you?'

⑬ Some of the users of the Afro-Caribbean Elders Day Centre are reluctant to reveal their ages. Michael, a former volunteer worker, was embarrassed about asking this, so he used to guess when filling in the database. After a talk by the council Welfare Rights Officer, the centre realises that some of their users could be claiming age-related benefits. Joyce, the centre manager, agrees that this use of data is within the original purpose, so she agrees to search the database for users over a specific age.

The first problem is that the database has been set up to record the age of the person when they first started using the centre. These ages have not been updated, so the centre is in danger of breaking the fourth Data Protection Principle: the data is not kept up to date. For now, the staff realise that they can work out the current ages by seeing how long the person has been a user, but for the future they decide to change the database so that it records date of birth and calculates the current age, rather than recording a specific age.

Then they find that some of the ages Michael has guessed turn out to be under-estimates. When Joyce pulls off a list of people to talk to about the benefits they may be entitled to, some of those who should be invited to the talk get missed off. These people find out that their friends are claiming a benefit that they are not, and some of them complain. This could be another breach of the fourth Data Protection Principle: the data is not accurate. Joyce decides to make it very clear to volunteers from now on that they must not guess. If they don't know the answer, they must leave the field blank or enter a specific 'don't know' value (and the database must be set up so that this is possible). In this way, if the centre is doing a similar exercise in future, the staff can make sure that those whose ages they don't know get invited to the talk as well.

5

Fair processing

Transparency is an essential component of good practice — unless the Data Subject knows what you are doing, they can't raise any concerns or objections.

This chapter looks at:

▶ The need to ensure that the Data Subject is informed, and the occasions when it is fair not to inform them

▶ The 'conditions' for fair processing and the circumstances in which you can process data without consent

If the Data Protection Act can be summed up in one sentence, it is probably in Principle 1: 'Personal data shall be processed fairly'. The Act goes into some detail about what this means.

Transparency

The main requirement for fair processing is transparency. If the Data Subject would be surprised to find out that you have data about them, or surprised by what you are doing with it, then you have almost certainly failed to be sufficiently transparent.

This transparency should extend to:

- the fact that you have information about the Data Subject;
- all the purposes that you use it for, especially any that are not obvious;
- who you might disclose it to;
- how the Data Subject can exercise any rights they have, to obtain information or to place restrictions on your use of the data.

You may provide this information in any appropriate way, but it has to be available before the Data Subject commits to giving you their information or, if you get it from someone else, as soon as reasonably practicable. Except in the cases discussed below, it is likely to be unfair to use data about people in any way without their knowledge, and without being open about who you are and how you can easily be contacted.

Processing

Processing has been defined in the 1998 Act effectively to include anything that may bring you into contact with personal data: from collecting it, through holding, using, changing, copying, disclosing or passing it on, all the way through to destroying or erasing it.

Processing

…means obtaining, recording or holding the information or data or carrying out any operation or set of operations on the information or data, including:

(**a**) organisation, adaptation or alteration of the information or data,

(**b**) retrieval, consultation or use of the information or data,

(**c**) disclosure of the information or data by transmission, dissemination or otherwise making available, or

(**d**) alignment, combination, blocking, erasure or destruction of the information or data.

Fair Processing Code

While all processing has to be fair, the Act is particularly concerned with how you collect or otherwise obtain personal data. In expanding on Principle 1, the Act sets out the Fair Processing Code. This spells out several things that you have to do. Without them processing is automatically unfair. But this leaves the Data Controller with a general responsibility for fairness above and beyond the specific requirements of the Code.

The Code makes it clear in particular that data has not been collected fairly if:

- anyone has been deceived or misled in the process;
- the Data Subject does not know who is processing the data and what they intend to do with it.

In addition, the Data Subject has to have 'any further information which is necessary [in the circumstances] to enable processing … to be fair'. The 1995 European Directive gives examples of what this 'further' information might be. These include:

- the recipients or categories of recipients;
- whether data provision is voluntary or mandatory;
- the existence of the right of access.

This does not necessarily mean that you have to go to great lengths to tell people about why you are collecting their data: it may be obvious. When you take on a new member of staff and ask them for their bank details so that you can pay them, a Data Protection statement is likely to be superfluous.

However, you do have to take care where any intended use of the data is not immediately obvious. Even if you have specified the non-obvious purpose by notification to the Information Commissioner, you still have to ensure that the Data Subject knows what is going on before the processing can be fair. In particular you need to make the Data Subject aware if you intend to make any non-obvious disclosure to a third party – for example if some of the services you offer are actually delivered by someone else and you need to pass on member or client details for this to happen.

Many voluntary organisations' existing policies in areas such as client information and confidentiality will already go beyond the letter of the Data Protection requirements. However, in some cases practices may need to be changed, particularly where contact with clients is made over the telephone or through a third party acting on behalf of the organisation. The practical implications of this are discussed in Chapter 10.

Processing without the Data Subject's knowledge

Where you obtain personal data not directly from the Data Subject but from a third party, the Data Subject is still entitled to know who you are and what you are doing, unless this would require 'disproportionate effort'. This is almost the only ground on which the information may be withheld. See Chapter 10 for a discussion on this.

If you are relying on the 'disproportionate effort' exemption, you have to keep a record of your reasons for believing the argument applies.[12] You must also provide the information to anyone who asks for it. (Remember that this exemption does *not* apply to data you get directly from the Data Subject, only to data you obtain from someone else.)

> **My clients often give me details of people who have harassed them. I can't possibly tell the harassers that I'm holding data on them; it would put my clients in serious jeopardy.**
>
> This question has caused some debate. It appears likely that the Information Commissioner would accept an argument based on 'disproportionate effort' if telling the harasser amounted to a breach of confidentiality towards your client. It may also be relevant to look at the crime prevention exemption (see Chapter 13). Either way, you would not have to tell the harasser that you held data on them.
>
> You must, however, take account of the rights of all parties in this situation. If the risks were less serious, or if you did not have a duty of confidentiality to your client, you would be more likely to have to inform the third party.

---

[12] This rule has been added to the Act by Regulation (Statutory Instrument 2000 No. 185, paragraph 5).

> **Conditions relevant for purposes of the first principle: processing of any personal data (Schedule 2 of the Act)**
>
> 1 The data subject has given his consent to the processing.
> 2 The processing is necessary:
>   (a) for the performance of a contract to which the data subject is a party, or
>   (b) for the taking of steps at the request of the data subject with a view to entering into a contract.
> 3 The processing is necessary for compliance with any legal obligation to which the data controller is subject, other than an obligation imposed by contract.
> 4 The processing is necessary in order to protect the vital interests of the data subject.
> 5 The processing is necessary:
>   (a) for the administration of justice,
>   (b) for the exercise of any functions conferred on any person by or under any enactment,
>   (c) for the exercise of any functions of the Crown, a Minister of the Crown or a government department, or
>   (d) for the exercise of any other functions of a public nature exercised in the public interest by any person.
> 6 (1) The processing is necessary for the purposes of legitimate interests pursued by the data controller or by the third party or parties to whom the data are disclosed, except where the processing is unwarranted in any particular case by reason of prejudice to the rights and freedoms or legitimate interests of the data subject.
>   (2) The Secretary of State may by order specify particular circumstances in which this condition is, or is not, to be taken to be satisfied.

Conditions for fair processing

Principle 1 refers to the 'conditions' for fair processing that are set out in Schedule 2 of the Act, and are quoted in full in the box. Data processing is not considered fair unless it meets at least one of these conditions:

1 The Data Subject has given consent.
2 Processing is necessary to carry out a contract to which the Data Subject is a party.
3 Processing is necessary to meet a legal obligation of the Data Controller.
4 Processing is necessary to protect the vital interests of the Data Subject.

5 Processing is necessary for various judicial and government functions.
6 Processing is in the legitimate interests of the Data Controller – unless it causes harm to the Data Subject's rights, freedoms or legitimate interests.

The first condition, consent, is discussed in Chapter 7. For the other conditions, 2 to 6, the processing must be 'necessary' for the stated purpose. It is up to the Data Controller to judge in the first place what is necessary.

The Information Commissioner has indicated that 'vital interests' (Condition 4) will be interpreted very narrowly, as 'life or death' emergencies. She does not want to see it used routinely. Many voluntary organisations may want to make the case that situations such as actual or potential homelessness, harassment, abuse and threats of serious violence are also 'vital interests'. As things stand, however, this is not the Information Commissioner's interpretation (see also the next chapter).

While all processing has to meet at least one of the six conditions, not all instances of processing the same set of data need meet the same condition.

- Data collected with consent might subsequently be used without consent to protect the vital interests of the Data Subject, provided that this is compatible with the original purpose for which it was collected.
- Data collected in connection with a contract might be used in the interests of the Data Controller (for example if staff details were provided to an employer's liability insurer), again provided that this was compatible with the purpose(s) specified at the time when the data was obtained.
- Some people on a contact database may have given consent (by asking to be kept in touch), while others may be there on the grounds of the Data Controller's legitimate interests (for example because they are local councillors), without having consented.

> **We do a lot of work under contract to the council. Are we carrying out 'functions of a public nature' and therefore covered by Condition 5(d)?**
>
> Probably not. Following a court case in 2002 involving the Leonard Cheshire Foundation, it appears that even where a voluntary organisation is providing statutory services under contract to a local authority, this does not amount to carrying out a 'public function' in relation to the Human Rights Act 1998. It would be logical to assume that the same would apply to the similar terms in the Data Protection Act.

It is very hard to envisage any reasonable activity in most voluntary organisations which would fail to meet at least one of the conditions. The requirement to meet the conditions is therefore unlikely to impose any major burden. The important point is that the Data Controller must be able to say, if the question is raised, which condition (or conditions) they are relying on.

Summary

All processing of personal data must meet at least one of six conditions. It must take place:

- with the consent of the Data Subject; or
- in connection with a contract involving the Data Subject; or
- to meet a legal obligation; or
- to protect the Data Subject's 'vital interests'; or
- to fulfil a wide range of government functions; or
- in your 'legitimate interests', provided that the Data Subject is not harmed.

EXAMPLES

⑭ The staff of a sheltered-housing scheme find that some of the residents are being bombarded with marketing material after filling in a 'lifestyle questionnaire'. They decide to help the residents complain on the grounds that the residents were misled about the purpose of the survey, and that the processing of their data is therefore unfair.

⑮ A council for voluntary service maintains a database of local organisations, with details of contact people. The information officer, Jane, is unsure whether she can keep these contact names without consent. She is quickly reassured that this use of the data is likely to fall under Condition 6: it is in the legitimate interests of the Data Controller and the Data Subjects are not being harmed (they gave their names voluntarily as contact people, after all). However, if the CVS were in the business of publishing a directory of local organisations, it would need to consider whether those contact people who had given their home address, for example, could be included without consent. The details of the organisations themselves, of course, are not covered by Data Protection.

⑯ Barry is the secretary of a small charitable trust which gives money to individuals in the locality. He keeps a list of beneficiaries on his computer and has been complying with the Data Protection Act as a Data Controller. Then his trust decides to merge with another one. The new organisation is technically a new Data Controller, but the committee decides not to contact previous beneficiaries of either trust whose records are now in the new combined archive, on the grounds of disproportionate effort. They minute this decision, so that it is on record.

For further examples of the Fair Processing Code in operation, see Chapter 10.

6

Processing sensitive personal data

The special categories of 'sensitive' data have to meet additional, more stringent, conditions before you can process them fairly. Often this means that you will need consent from the Data Subject.

This chapter looks at:

▶ The circumstances when you do and do not need consent to process sensitive data

'Sensitive' data, as defined in the Act (see box), is subject to special rules. The definition is quoted here in full and has omissions that may cause surprise. Although details of personal finances, and other data such as age or date of birth, may well be felt by some people to be highly sensitive, it is important to draw the distinction between these personal assessments and the actual requirements of the law.

Sensitive personal data[13]

is personal data consisting of information as to:

(a) the racial or ethnic origin of the data subject,

(b) his[14] political opinions,

(c) his religious beliefs or other beliefs of a similar nature,

(d) whether he is a member of a trade union (within the meaning of the Trade Union and Labour Relations (Consolidation) Act 1992),

(e) his physical or mental health or condition,

(f) his sexual life,

(g) the commission or alleged commission by him of any offence, or

(h) any proceedings for any offence committed or alleged to have been committed by him, the disposal of such proceedings or the sentence of any Court in such proceedings.

---

[13] See paragraph 2 of the Act.
[14] UK legislation is not yet written in a gender-neutral way. Where the Act itself is quoted, 'he', 'him' and 'his' apply equally to women.

Data Protection Principle 1 states that any Data Controller processing sensitive personal data has to meet at least one of the conditions in Schedule 3. This is summarised here, and quoted in full in Appendix B. In addition to the Schedule itself, the Home Secretary has powers to extend the list of conditions. This has been done under Regulations,[15] which are taken into account in the discussion that follows.

In order to process sensitive data, you have to meet at least one of the conditions. For voluntary organisations, the most likely to apply include:

- You have the Data Subject's 'explicit' consent.
- You have a legal obligation to process the data in connection with employment.
- It is in the 'vital interests' of the Data Subject or another person, and either consent cannot be obtained or it is reasonable to proceed without it.
- You are processing membership data in certain non-profit associations, but *not* most charities or voluntary organisations.
- The data has been made public deliberately by the Data Subject.
- You need to process the data in connection with giving legal advice or defending legal rights.
- You need to process the data in connection with medical care and have a medical practitioner's duty of confidentiality.
- You are processing data about ethnic or racial origin, disability or religion in order to monitor equal opportunities.
- You need to process the data in order to provide confidential counselling, advice, support or other services, and either consent cannot be obtained or it is reasonable to proceed without it.

Other conditions relate to insurance and police activities, for example. The intention is clearly that in most cases a Data Controller should aim to meet the **first condition**, which is to have the 'explicit' consent of the Data Subject. 'Explicit' is not defined, and guidance from the Information Commissioner suggests only that explicit consent may need to be clearer and more detailed than the consent which may be sought for processing non-sensitive data (see following chapter).

You can process sensitive personal data *without* the Data Subject's explicit consent only if one of the other conditions applies. In the rest of this chapter, we will look at these, and circumstances in which they might apply, one by one. If you believe that any of these conditions might apply, consult Appendix B for the full definition.

---

[15] Statutory Instrument 2000 No. 417.

Processing sensitive data without consent

The **second condition** provides for processing which is necessary for the purposes of complying with the law in connection with employment. This is a very narrow definition. It is standard employment practice, for example, to hold much more information about an employee's health than is strictly required by law. It appears that there may be a conflict between this and Data Protection, since consent is rarely sought. This will be covered in Part 4 of the Information Commissioner's Employment Code of Practice, which was not available at the time of writing.

> **We have a wall chart in our office, showing staff absences. Colour codes indicate the reason for the absence, including 'sick'. Is this OK?**
>
> Quite possibly not. The fact that someone is sick is sensitive personal data, and they may not want their colleagues to draw adverse conclusions. (Equally, the environment may be very supportive and they are happy for their colleagues to know exactly what is wrong; but that should be the Data Subject's choice.)
>
> An alternative would be to mark them as 'out of the office', so that colleagues know to take messages and so on, but for only the line manager to know whether this is due to illness, a course, a meeting, working from home or waiting in for the gas engineer.

The **third condition** has been the subject of much debate. It allows processing that is necessary in order to protect the vital interests of the Data Subject *or another person,* in cases where consent cannot be obtained or where it is reasonable to proceed without it.

> **We want to use the third condition in order to keep a database of known sex offenders who are deemed unsuitable to work with our vulnerable clients. Is this OK?**
>
> Probably not. The Information Commissioner views 'vital interests' as meaning life or death only, and has also pointed out other potential problems with such a proposal – for example the difficulty in being sure that you have identified people correctly and recorded the details sufficiently accurately. A Criminal Records Bureau check is much more likely to be the appropriate course of action (see Appendix C).

The **fourth condition** allows non-profit organisations with religious, political, trade union or philosophical aims to process sensitive data about their members, or people in regular contact with the organisation, subject to certain safeguards. This is permitted because, by their nature, such organisations will inevitably hold sensitive data. Verbal guidance from the Information Commissioner's staff confirms that 'philosophical' aims do not cover the activities of most charities or voluntary organisations. An equivalent provision for medical self-help groups would be logical, but does not seem to be on the cards.

The **fifth condition** covers sensitive data which the Data Subject has deliberately made public. You would not, for example, need consent to record the political affiliation of someone who had stood as a candidate for a specific party.

The **sixth condition** allows sensitive data to be processed without consent where it is necessary in connection with legal proceedings, obtaining legal advice, or establishing, exercising or defending legal rights. While an agency giving legal advice would normally have no problem getting consent from clients, this could allow data about third parties to be held without their consent in connection with a broad range of legal advice work.

The **seventh condition** is very similar to the equivalent condition in Schedule 2, exempting government functions from the need to obtain consent for processing sensitive data, but it lacks the provision for 'functions of a public nature' exercised by others.

> ### Our equal opportunities monitoring cannot be done anonymously. Do we need consent?
>
> Normally, no. However, if you do not seek consent you *must* make it clear that providing the information is optional, and you *must not* use the information for any purpose other than equal opportunities.
>
> Monitoring on grounds of racial or ethnic origin, disability or religion (which are all sensitive data) are given specific provision, while age, gender or other grounds such as where people live are not sensitive data and you could argue that it is in your legitimate interests. You should be more careful where you are asking about sexuality or criminal record, as there is no special provision for these, and they are 'sensitive'.

The **eighth condition** relates to processing sensitive data where it is necessary for medical purposes, but only where this is done by a health professional, or someone who owes an equivalent duty of confidentiality. 'Medical purposes' is defined quite widely, to include care as well as treatment. However, it does not apply to employers seeking medical references from potential employees. The employer would need the Data Subject's consent for this use of their medical records.

The **ninth condition** makes specific provision to permit processing of sensitive data about ethnic or racial origin where this is aimed at promoting equal opportunities. Among the **additional conditions** which have been added by Regulation are ones providing for the use of information on disability or religion for equalities monitoring. In these cases the Regulation states specifically that the information must not be used for making decisions about individuals.

Among the other **additional conditions** is one allowing processing of sensitive data for the provision of confidential counselling, advice, support or other services, provided that certain safeguards are met. The processing must be in the 'substantial public interest', and it is only permissible if, in addition:

- consent cannot be obtained, or
- it is unreasonable to obtain consent, or
- seeking consent would jeopardise the provision of the service.

This does simplify matters in a number of tricky areas where the Data Subjects may be distressed or otherwise unable to give meaningful consent. It may be more honest to use this condition than to obtain spurious 'consent'. For example, a voluntary organisation providing support to carers might well be able to hold information about the medical condition of the person being cared for without their consent (which may well be impossible or unreasonable to obtain). A counselling service might well be able to record allegations of abuse without seeking the consent of the alleged abuser.

Can sensitive data be implied? If someone is the contact for the local Sikh gurdwara does that mean I am holding information about their religious beliefs?

A common-sense approach is probably required. If the circumstances suggest that the individual definitely falls into a particular category where the data would be sensitive, then treat it as such. Think about whether you actually need the data in question, and whether you can make any disclosures in a less revealing way. (Don't forget that where data has been made deliberately public, the conditions are met.)

In many cases you cannot make the assumption. People may sign up to receive mailings about a particular medical condition without having it themselves, for example. This list would therefore not be sensitive.

Summary

In order to process 'sensitive' personal data, you must meet at least one of the following conditions. Your processing must:

- be with the 'explicit' consent of the Data Subject;
- be necessary to meet legal requirements in connection with employment;
- be necessary to protect the vital interests of the Data Subject or another person;
- concern the membership records of certain specified non-profit membership associations;
- involve information deliberately publicised by the Data Subject;
- be in connection with legal advice or protecting legal rights;
- be in connection with a range of government functions;
- be necessary to provide medical care;
- concern equalities monitoring on race/ethnicity, disability or religion;
- be necessary in connection with confidential counselling, advice or support work;
- be in connection with the provision of insurance, or certain other situations.

In most cases there are limitations to the extent to which the conditions may be fulfilled. See Appendix B for the full details.

EXAMPLES

⑰ Veronica runs the fundraising department for a small medical charity. Quite often people write in with a donation and mention in the accompanying letter that the reason they are giving the donation is because they themselves have the medical condition in question. Veronica would like to keep this information on file for when she writes back in future, and wonders whether the fifth condition in Schedule 3 might apply: has the information been made 'deliberately public' by the Data Subject, or does she need to go back and get explicit consent?

She telephones the Information Commissioner's office where she is told that in their view the letter does not count as being 'public'. So if Veronica does want to keep the information she will need to satisfy one of the other conditions. In this case that almost certainly means phoning or writing back to get explicit consent.

(18) Maddy is the Manager of a carers' support project. Her volunteers visit carers at home, and in the course of their work pick up a lot of information about not just the carer but also the person they are caring for. Some of this information is 'sensitive', such as information about the medical condition of the person being cared for.

Maddy's approach is twofold. First she has to make sure that she records only information that she genuinely needs. She consults the volunteers and they reach an agreement about the types of information that need to go into the files, both for the organisation's own monitoring and so that volunteers can pass on to each other the information they need in order to provide the services.

Secondly, some of this information does relate to the medical condition of the person being cared for, and is therefore 'sensitive' personal data. The agency workers decide that they are able to guarantee confidentiality, and that many of the people being cared for would not be in a position to give consent. They will therefore hold this information under the 'confidential services' condition.

A colleague of Maddy's, Thomas, faces a slightly different situation. His volunteers are involved in mediation and they sometimes have to visit households where some of the residents have a history of criminal violence. For the safety of the volunteers, Thomas feels that it is essential that they are aware of situations like this and, again, that it may not be appropriate to seek consent. He decides to take advice on whether he can use the same argument as Maddy or rely on the third condition, 'protecting vital interests'.

Data Subject consent

One of the most important questions you have to answer is whether you need consent for the uses you make of people's data.

This chapter looks at:

▶ All the questions surrounding consent and how to obtain it

'Consent' is not defined in the 1998 Data Protection Act. Guidance from the Information Commissioner, based on the EU Directive from which the Act is derived, indicates that consent has to be 'freely given, specific and informed', and the Data Subject has to 'signify' their wishes.

This would mean that consent can be inferred from something the Data Subject does, but not from something they don't do. In other words, if the Data Subject knows fully what is going to be done with their data and goes ahead with providing it, they can be taken to have consented. However, if you mail people saying 'we'll keep you on our database unless you tell us otherwise' the Information Commissioner's view is that you don't have consent from those who don't reply, because they haven't done anything.

The Commissioner is not necessarily right, and her guidance does not have the force of law. There is an opposing legal opinion that if, for example, you are already in contact with people it might be sufficient to invite them to consent, give them easy ways to object, but then inform them that you will assume consent if you have not heard back within a given period. You could also inform them that you will continue to process their data under the sixth Condition ('legitimate interests') unless they specifically tell you not to. This issue will undoubtedly be the subject of further debate. The discussion below adheres to the Commissioner's line.

Although the consent must be 'freely given' you are allowed to explain the direct consequences of not consenting. For example, 'Without your National Insurance number we can't find out what has happened to your benefits claim.'

Data obtained from the Data Subject

When you collect information on paper, or on an electronic form, you will often be in a position to provide all the information that the Data Subject needs in order to decide whether to give consent. It may be completely obvious from the context who will use the data being collected and what for, for example on a booking form, an order form or an application form, where the name of the organisation collecting the data will be prominent and the purpose clear. You may want to reinforce this by providing a short Data Protection statement ensuring that the Data Subject is in no doubt. If they go ahead and fill in the

---

Does consent have to be in writing?

No. Verbal consent is just as valid as written consent. The only issue is whether you feel you need evidence that consent was given. In many cases, you may not feel any need for evidence. Suppose, for example, you have a client in front of you and you ask: 'Is it OK if I pass your details on to organisation X so that they can help you?' When they say 'Yes', you make the phone call, and that's it.

On the other hand, you may feel that it would be safer to have evidence, in case the Data Subject's understanding and yours diverge in future. A signature on a piece of paper is one solution, provided the Data Subject signed in the full knowledge of what they were getting into. Alternatives would include:

- Obtaining verbal consent, then writing to the Data Subject to confirm what you have agreed, and giving them the option to raise any disagreement.
- Being able to demonstrate that you have consistent procedures for obtaining informed consent, which are regularly checked and monitored.
- Making an entry in the record at the time to confirm that you have obtained consent. Your data collection forms could be adapted to give a space for this.
- Making the consent box on screen mandatory with no default: in other words anyone filling in the form on screen cannot proceed without actively entering yes or no.
- Asking a sample of clients whether their consent was actively sought and properly explained.

Whatever you decide to do, you must make sure that all your staff and volunteers understand when they need to get clear consent, and know how to do it.

---

form, and you are happy that they know exactly what they are letting themselves in for, you can take it that you have their consent.

You may be in the same situation when people give you information face to face or over the phone. If they have initiated the contact – by visiting your agency or phoning you up – they have done something specific and, again provided you are sure that they have all the information they need, you may be able to assume consent. If the contact is trivial you may need to say nothing: they phone up to order a free brochure and you record their address merely in order to get the brochure sent out when it is published in two weeks' time. Provided you won't keep the information after that, or use it for something else, they know all they need to know.

In other cases you may need to be more specific, or even to check that you do have their consent. For example, you may need to say, 'Do you mind if we keep your details so that we can let you know if we publish any other material on the same topic?'

When the contact is the beginning of a closer relationship, such as when you take on a new client, you are likely to spend time explaining the arrangements anyway. It is particularly easy if you need them to sign something at this stage, agreeing to the service you are providing. You can build consent for your use of their data into the statement they sign.

Data not obtained from the Data Subject

Where you obtain data from a third party you are obviously not in a position to get consent from the Data Subject. Although they may originally have given the organisation or individual that is the source of the data consent to disclose it, this is not the same as giving you consent to use it (because consent must be 'specific'). If you need or want their consent, you have to seek it directly.

Data you hold already

You might be holding information that you obtained a long time ago without seeking consent. Do you need to do anything? It depends on the circumstances.

If the data is used for something that involves the Data Subject in doing something, you probably don't need to take any specific action. For example, if they renew their membership annually, the fact that they return their membership renewal is likely to count as consent. Of course, you mustn't use the data for anything they wouldn't expect as a member. You would need to look at the information they were provided with when they originally signed up, or which you had sent them since.

If the data is being kept for historical purposes – old client records, for example – the main requirement is for you to be sure that you are not keeping it for longer than necessary. Provided you are satisfied on this, then it is probably in your legitimate interests to keep the data, and the Data Subject is not being harmed. If so, you do not need to seek consent.

A more complex area is the type of database where you may need to contact people infrequently, but there is no regular relationship. This could include, for example, a list of people who receive your Annual Report, or a list of people who you hope may give you money in the future (and who may have given in the past) but who are not currently active donors. If you follow the Information Commissioner's guidance you cannot just write to say 'tell us if you want to come off the database'. That may be a worthwhile action in its own right, but it does not solve your problem because a non-response would *not count* as consent according to the Commissioner.

The first consideration here is to make sure that everyone on the database knows that you are holding their data and why. If the names are just sitting there and not being used there is a risk that you are holding them longer than necessary. If you are not using the information, why are you holding it? If, however, you decide that you do have a legitimate interest in continuing to hold the data, then you do not necessarily need consent (for example, if you are planning a centenary appeal to all your old members in a few years' time). In any case, it is worth making sure that you do contact everyone on the list at some stage to ensure that they know you have the data, and to tell them how to get taken off your database if this is what they want.

'Explicit' consent for sensitive data

When you need explicit consent, you cannot assume that you have it merely from the fact that someone goes ahead with providing information. You need to spell out why you need the data and how you will use it, including any safeguards that you will apply, and any self-imposed restrictions on disclosures (such as not making any disclosure without the Data Subject's consent).

> ### Does 'explicit' consent have to be in writing?
> No. You may want to get it in writing, so that you can demonstrate that you have provided all the information required. You could have a statement for people to sign saying, 'I have read the information above about how the centre uses my information, and I am happy for this to happen.' But the important thing is to provide the explicit information before asking for the data.

Where the Data Subject is providing information on a paper form and is signing a statement anyway you can incorporate their consent into the statement. Applicants for a job may be undertaking that the statements they have given on the form are true. New clients may be asking you to take on a particular piece of work, and possibly giving you permission to act for them. Parents may be authorising you to take their children on outings or to administer medicine in emergencies. In any of these cases it is relatively easy to add a sentence to the statement they sign, inviting the person to give explicit consent for any processing of sensitive data.

The same principles could be applied to an electronic form, with appropriate safeguards to verify the identity of the individual.

The most important consideration when you are getting consent for the use of sensitive data is to be very explicit about why you want it and how you will use it. For example, the booking forms for your training courses might say: 'Is there anything we can do to help you participate fully in the course? (See brochure for what we can offer.) Any information you give us here will be passed only to the course tutor and/or relevant staff so that they can make appropriate arrangements. We will not retain this information after the course.' Anyone who then provides you with information about their health, for example, has consented to that use.

> ### At what age can children consent on their own behalf?
> In Scotland the Act lays down that children are deemed able to consent from the age of 12. In England and Wales the test is different: you have to decide on a case by case basis whether the child is capable of fully understanding what they are being asked to consent to. By analogy with Scotland this is quite likely to be around the age of 12.

Consent is not necessarily universal or permanent

The Information Commissioner has expressed the view that the Data Subject may be entitled to consent to some of the things you want to do with their data but at the same time to withhold consent from others. For example, if Data Subjects need to provide information in order to receive a service they are likely to consent to that. But if you also intend to use the information for other purposes you may need to get consent for these separately. In particular you may need specific consent for disclosing data to someone else if this is not connected with the main purpose for which the information is being obtained by you.

> **We collect information in order to run our training courses. We also want to use data about our course participants for other purposes – for example we would like to take pictures of the participants, to use in our courses brochure. Is it enough just to tell people that this is what we do?**
>
> Probably not. If you want to use data for a secondary purpose, you probably need consent. It would not be fair otherwise, and if you don't give people a genuine choice then their consent has not been 'freely given'. It would be different if the two purposes were inextricably linked – for example if the photos were a necessary part of the course work. In that case, provided you tell people about it, the choice is then theirs to sign up for the course or not.

Because consent must be 'freely given' you would not be able to say, 'We will provide our main service only on condition that you give consent for us to use the information that we collect for a secondary purpose as well.' This means that you should give people the chance to opt out: 'We would also like to pass your details to other organisations offering services you might be interested in. If you do not want us to do this, please tick here ☐'.

Data Subjects may also withdraw consent. If you are relying on consent for meeting the fair processing conditions (in Schedule 2) and the Data Subject then decides to withdraw their consent, it would quite possibly be unfair to carry on using the data under one of the other conditions, even if you could genuinely meet one or more of them.

> **Can one person consent on behalf of another?**
>
> Yes, but only under certain conditions. The person giving consent must be properly authorised, and must be acting in the Data Subject's interests. Ideally you would be looking for formal, legal authorisation:
>
> - A parent can consent on behalf of a child who is too young to give consent on their own behalf.
> - Someone with a power of attorney can make decisions on someone else's behalf.
>
> If neither of these cases applies, you need to be confident that the person acting on behalf of the Data Subject really is authorised. If in any doubt you should ask to see a signed authorisation from the Data Subject.
>
> Where you are working with adults who cannot give consent, or where you do not feel able to seek consent, you may feel it is more honest to meet one of the conditions for processing without consent, rather than getting a meaningless signature.

Summary

- Consent to use personal data must be specific, informed and freely given.
- Consent need not be in writing.
- Consent can normally be implied from something the Data Subject does, but not from anything they fail to do.
- For 'explicit' consent to process sensitive data, you must explain carefully why you need the information and what you will do with it.

EXAMPLES

⑲ Miles runs a membership organisation. Every year members get a letter asking them to renew their subscription. He decides to include on the letter a statement that members' data will be used only for administering member activities and benefits. He reasons that if members go ahead and send the form back, they have consented to this use of their data.

However, someone on the committee then proposes publishing a county-by-county list of members, so that they can get in touch with each other. Before the plan is put into action, Miles points out that this is a new venture; people may not have realised that it would be one of the member services to be undertaken, so they cannot be said to have consented to it.

The whole project is shelved until members can be asked, both in principle at the AGM and individually, whether they want their details made public in this way.

⑳ Sue's advice agency has a strict confidentiality policy. When new clients sign up, they are always told that there are a very few circumstances when the centre is legally obliged to break confidentiality, but that otherwise no disclosures will be made without their consent. Whenever the client visits the centre, staff are careful to ask for consent before making any referrals. However, if they need to consult specialist colleagues about a case they do not seek consent if the consultation can take place without identifying the client, since this does not involve disclosing personal data, and is not a breach of confidentiality.

8

How long should data be kept?

The fifth Data Protection Principle says that data must not be held longer than 'necessary', but many people find it hard to assess what this means. There are also exemptions which apply to archives and historical material.

This chapter covers:

▶ The issues that apply to retention of archives

▶ The use of records for historical or statistical purposes

There is no simple rule for deciding when to destroy, erase or archive data. Each situation is different, depending on what is *necessary* for the purpose(s) for which you hold the data. The questions you may wish to ask include:

- Is there a legal time limit for holding this data? For example, some records relating to occupational health now have to be held for 40 years. Information on employment selection should be held for about six months in case an unsuccessful candidate should bring a claim of discrimination, but need not be held any longer than that.
- Do you have specific advice from professionals? For instance, your indemnity insurer may want you to keep detailed client records for as long as a negligence claim might be valid.
- Has the reason for holding the data changed? When a member of staff leaves, it might be the appropriate time to reduce their file to those items you must archive long term or permanently.
- Do you know for a fact that the information is out of date? If mail gets returned, you would have a hard job to justify keeping an address that you know is wrong.
- Is the data used according to a routine rhythm? If you mail people to ask for money twice a year, you may want to set a specific number of non-responses after which you will assume that they have lost interest.
- Can you confidently describe the next time you are going to use the data? If not, it may have outstayed its welcome. Keeping information 'just in case' is

not only a waste of your storage space; it is unlikely to be satisfactory Data Protection practice.

A good rule of thumb is to try to imagine any circumstance in which you might be asked to produce the data. If not having the data would matter, then there is clear justification for keeping it. If there is no possibility of being asked for it, or if being unable to produce it wouldn't matter, then there is a strong case for erasing or destroying it.

You should also consider the question of how much the Data Subject knows about your retention policy. If you tell job applicants at the time they apply that their details will be held in case a suitable vacancy comes up in the future, then you are far less likely to be contravening the Principle than if you leave them with the impression that you are only concerned with the single current vacancy.

When the time does come to destroy material, remember that erasure or destruction is still 'processing', so it must still comply with the Principles, including fairness and security. Where you hold highly confidential data you may want to think about using a program to make it irrecoverable from your computer or disk, or about secure destruction methods such as shredding. What you do not want is to throw material away, only for it to turn up blowing around in the street outside your office.

Research, history and statistics

Even when you have finished using data for its original purpose, if you have a valid reason for keeping it, you do not necessarily have to dispose of it. There is an exemption allowing data to be processed for research, history and statistics, even if this was not the original reason for its collection. Under this exemption the data may be kept indefinitely and may be used regardless of the purpose(s) it was originally obtained for, provided that:

- the processing does not support actions or decisions relating to specific individuals *and*
- the processing does not cause anyone substantial damage or distress.

You may decide that your archives are of such potential interest in the future – perhaps to researchers, or even to your Data Subjects if you hold information about key events in their lives – that you can easily justify keeping them. It might even be fairer to the Data Subject to keep the information. You should, however, be careful to distinguish between 'live' information and 'historical' archives, and ensure that access to the historical material is suitably restricted.

Statistical material, of course, once individual Data Subjects are no longer identifiable, is not subject to Data Protection restrictions on disclosure, because it has ceased to be personal data. If there is no reason to keep the material in such a way that the Data Subject is still identifiable, you may find it more appropriate to convert it into an anonymous form.

Transitional protection for manual archives

Following the introduction of the Act, there was a transitional period for existing activities to be brought into line. This expired on 24 October 2001, meaning that virtually all processing of personal data has had to be fully compliant since then.

There is, however, a remaining transitional period of six years – to 23 October 2007 – before manual data which was *held before 24 October 1998* has to comply with the Data Protection Principles regarding quality of data (the third, fourth and fifth Principles) and various other provisions of the new Act. This provides time to sort out your archives, but it is important to ensure that *any* information added to a manual system after 23 October 1998, even a pre-existing one, complies with the new Act immediately.

Archives are *not* exempt from Subject Access during the transitional period. Anyone making a Subject Access request would be entitled to see all your historical material about themselves as well as current records.

Summary

- You cannot continue to keep data without a good reason.
- Take advice on appropriate retention periods from relevant professionals where possible.
- Otherwise, make your own judgement, based on whether you can foresee any point in the future when you would genuinely need the information.
- If you want to keep information longer than the Data Subject might expect, make sure you let them know.
- There are exemptions allowing material to be held indefinitely for research or historical purposes, subject to certain conditions, even if this was not the original purpose.
- You may have until October 2007 to get your manual archives fully compliant, but they are not exempt from Subject Access in the interim.

9

Restrictions on fundraising and direct marketing

Data Subjects now have the right to prevent you from contacting them with a wide range of unsolicited material, but there is considerable debate over this provision. When you assist others with their marketing – through exchange of mailing lists, for example – there are further points to consider.

This chapter:

▶ Looks in detail at the requirements of the Act in respect of Data Subjects and unsolicited material

▶ Discusses the areas still in contention

▶ Covers the related Telecommunications (Data Protection and Privacy) Regulations 1999

For the first time in the UK, the Act gives individuals the right to prevent the use of their data for direct marketing. In this context 'direct marketing' must be taken to include much charity fundraising, as well as many other unsolicited approaches to Data Subjects. Although the onus is on the Data Subject to exercise this right, 'fairness' in processing is likely to require the provision of more information about how data is to be used, as well as the use of opt-out boxes on many leaflets and forms.

This is a significant new right, and should enable people to stem, or at least reduce, the flow of 'junk mail' where they wish to. Organisations that have not already adopted good practice in allowing people to opt out of direct marketing will have to make considerable changes.

What is direct marketing?

The definition of direct marketing in the Act is broad. It is the unsolicited 'communication (by whatever means) of any advertising or marketing material which is directed to particular individuals'. At its narrowest this will cover the marketing of goods or publications, distribution of a mail-order catalogue, or promotion of services such as training or other events. The Information Commissioner and many practitioners, however, interpret the definition far more broadly. It is generally accepted that any type of fundraising is covered. More controversially, the definition probably also includes a wide range of other activities which are designed in some way to promote the organisation, yet which also benefit the Data Subject.

In the commercial context this makes sense. Few commercial organisations would bother making unsolicited contact with Data Subjects unless there was ultimately something in it for the organisation. Voluntary organisations, however, are much more likely to act altruistically – sending out information which is wholly for the Data Subject's benefit, for example – or where the benefit to the organisation is marginal compared with the benefit to the Data Subject.

At the time of writing, there has been no case law which might clarify the definition. Onerous though it may seem in some instances, the most cautious approach is to class any unsolicited contact as direct marketing unless it clearly has no spin-off benefit for the Data Controller.

If the law were to accept this approach, direct marketing would include, for example:

- sending a book of raffle tickets to buy or sell;
- inviting someone to a free event designed to promote the organisation;
- sending out membership reminders, asking people to renew their membership;
- asking a previous donor to sign up to Gift Aid.

> **A lot of the time our fundraising department doesn't ask people for money, they just send people information in order to build and develop a relationship with them. This doesn't count as marketing, does it?**
>
> The reason why marketing receives special treatment in the Data Protection Act is because many people do regard a lot of the material they receive as 'junk mail' and would prefer not to receive it. Best practice, and the safest option, is to regard anything that is sent on your initiative as marketing, even if it doesn't ask for money or support, unless the information it contains is clearly for the direct benefit of the recipient, with no spin-off benefit for you. However, if you find this approach too restrictive, there are many areas around the fringes of marketing where you could probably make the opposite case. You do have to consider, though, the recipient's likely response if you send them material after they have opted out of marketing.

Restrictions on direct marketing clearly apply to any form of contact, including (but not limited to) mail, phone calls, faxes and e-mail.

The material has to be advertising or marketing and directed to the individual. Therefore, it is hard to see how the restrictions would apply to:

- material purely for information, for example an update to a previous information request;
- a flyer or brochure inserted in every copy of a magazine or other mailing;
- advertisements within publications or on posters;
- marketing material sent to an organisation, even via a contact person, provided you are asking the organisation to respond.

There are those, however, who would argue that if it is physically possible to send a newsletter out without its marketing content, then the option to opt out should be available. Many organisations face this issue, for example when the marketing material – such as a Christmas card catalogue or a book of raffle tickets – is being sent out with a membership mailing, but on behalf of another part of the organisation, or even a separate but linked trading company.

The right to opt out of direct marketing

The Act provides that the Data Subject may 'require' the Data Controller in writing not to use their data for direct marketing. However, you cannot leave it entirely up to the Data Subject to take the initiative, because of your responsibility to be 'fair' when obtaining information.

If you are obtaining the information directly from the Data Subject, in order to be fair you should give them the opportunity to opt out there and then, preferably through having a box to tick if they don't want future contact (an

Our fundraising manager doesn't want to frighten people off by putting opt-out boxes on the membership form. He wants to give the information in a follow-up letter and leave it up to the Data Subject to get in touch. Is this OK?

Not really. You have to put as few obstacles in people's way as possible. European Directive 95/46/EC says that the Data Subject has the right to object 'free of charge' to direct marketing. If the person is filling in a form and could be given the option of ticking a box, it is not 'free of charge' to make them contact you separately in an alternative way. As a minimum, if you really don't want to put the opt-out box on your data capture forms, you could either give them a freepost card to return or a freephone number to call.

'opt-out box'). It is much less likely to be fair if you tell them that they have to send in a form or write to a separate address in order to opt out.

If you obtain the information from someone else, you need to make it clear as soon as you use the information (which in most cases will mean when you first contact the Data Subjects) that you are using it for direct marketing, and giving them the opportunity to opt out, or telling them how to opt out. Again, anything that puts unnecessary obstacles in their way (such as a premium-rate opt-out phone number) could well be unfair.

It would certainly be a contravention of the Act to use material for direct marketing if this was not one of your 'specified' purposes when you collected it.

> **When people have participated in an event, we assume that they will be interested in the same event again next year. Surely we don't have to tell them we're going to contact them again, and give them an opt-out?**
>
> You should. While you may be right in assuming that most people will be happy to be contacted next year, this still counts as marketing, so it does need an opt-out.

The opt-out applies only where the material is unsolicited. If you advertise something in your newsletter and someone phones up to ask for more information, you can send a brochure even if they are marked on your database for 'no direct marketing'.

Approaching someone who has given money in the past to ask for another donation counts as unsolicited direct marketing, but following up a specific transaction is not. If someone sends a donation but forgets to sign their donation cheque, there is nothing to stop you getting back to them on that specific point, even if they have opted out of direct marketing.

The importance of the marketing opt-out can be seen in relation to the electoral roll. There is a legal requirement to be on the electoral roll and it must be made public – usually by being available for consultation in libraries. Local authorities can recoup part of their costs by making the electoral roll available electronically to commercial organisations, which then use it for purposes such as credit checking and direct marketing.

The Representation of the People Act 2000 took account of Data Protection by making provision for electors to opt out of the disclosure of their details for these additional purposes, but the government did not implement the relevant section in time for the 2001 compilation of the roll. One local authority was taken to court[16] as a result of not having offered the opt-out, and lost.

From December 2002, councils will have two versions of the electoral roll: the full register will be used for electoral, crime prevention and other limited purposes, such as credit checking. The edited register will be available for sale to anyone. From October 2002, the forms filled in by electors include an opt-out box for those who do not want to appear in the edited register.

Trading companies, list swaps and marketing on behalf of other organisations

Where a charity has a linked trading company there are, in effect, two Data Controllers. They may operate independently or they may, if they have access to a common database, be joint Data Controllers of the same data. Either way, it is necessary for each Data Controller to ensure that the Data Subject knows that their data is going to be used by the other.

Many voluntary organisations also exchange data for marketing purposes, either by swapping lists, by carrying out reciprocal mailings, or by enclosing other organisations' marketing material in with their own mailings.

'Trading/sharing in personal information' is a standard purpose, described by the Information Commissioner as 'the sale, hire, exchange or disclosure of personal data to third parties in return for goods/services/benefit'. This means that any kind of list swap is likely to be covered *even if the data itself is not disclosed.* (If you do a reciprocal mailing for someone else you would be exchanging your data in return for a benefit to you.) Where the other party is your own trading company, there is still a strong possibility that you are trading in personal data because 'you' are giving 'them' data in return for the funds 'they' raise.

This means that you must consider whether to include 'Trading/sharing in personal information' as one of the purposes in your notification (see Chapter 17); it is not an 'exempt' purpose. More importantly, you must ensure that your Data Subjects are made aware that their data will be passed to another Data Controller for marketing purposes, *and* you must give them the chance to opt out of this use.

Wherever possible this should be done at the time you obtain information from your Data Subjects, and preferably with an opt-out box on the form, along the lines of 'We would also like to send you material from our trading company' or 'From time to time we will send material from (or 'we will pass your name to') other organisations we believe you will be interested in', and in each case finishing off with 'If you do not want us to do this, please tick this box ☐'.

---

[16] The 'Robertson' case. R -v- City of Wakefield Metropolitan Council & another *ex parte* Robertson (16 November 2001).

> **Our sponsored events people want to pass on the names of participants to our fundraising department. Can they do this?**
>
> If the transfer is within one Data Controller, then it depends on what you told people you would do with their data. Provided the event sign-up form was clear that the data might be used for future marketing, and gave them an opt-out, then it doesn't matter which part of the organisation they hear from.

The Telecommunications (Data Protection and Privacy) Regulations 1999

A separate piece of legislation, the Telecommunications (Data Protection and Privacy) Regulations 1999,[17] gives additional rights with respect to marketing carried out by telephone. These Regulations are also enforced by the Information Commissioner.

The Regulations allow an individual[18] subscriber to 'notify' a caller that they don't want any further telemarketing calls from them. This 'notification' does not have to be in writing. Essentially you can tell anyone who rings with a marketing call 'Don't call again', and that should be sufficient. The definition of marketing is essentially the same as in the Data Protection Act.

The Regulations also put the Telephone Preference Service (TPS) on a statutory basis. Any individual subscriber can (in theory) prevent unwanted marketing calls by registering their phone number. Before any person or organisation makes a marketing call they must check the number they intend to ring against the register. If the number is on the register, direct marketing calls must not be made to it. It doesn't matter whether the number is from your own database, from someone else's list, from the phone book or dialled at random.

A phone number can be added to the register by phone. The number to call, at the time of writing, is 0845 070 0707. Information is also available from the operator and is given near the front of up-to-date telephone directories.

The register can be checked in a number of ways. The national register, or sub-sets of it, may be obtained in electronic format for a fee. (See **Further information** at the end of this book for details.) Alternatively, if you are using the services of a bureau to make calls for you, they should be able to check your list of numbers as part of the service, or you could use the services of a specialist 'list cleanser'.

The only way to make marketing calls without checking the register is if you already have permission for this from the person you are calling. For practical

---

[17] Statutory Instrument 1999 No. 2093.

[18] 'Individual' in this connection includes not only phone lines held in the name of individuals, but also those held in the name of unincorporated voluntary organisations and businesses, such as law firms, accountancy firms, surveyors, etc.

reasons, it is likely that consent for marketing calls would continue in operation, even if the subscriber subsequently put their number on the register. It may be worth pointing this out to people when seeking their consent for telemarketing.

The Regulations also forbid sending unsolicited faxes to individuals' lines unless they have given permission in advance. Businesses can prevent unwanted marketing faxes by registering with the Fax Preference Service (on 0845 070 0702) which operates on similar lines to the Telephone Preference Service.

Web and e-mail marketing and fundraising

Electronic commerce is the subject of additional European legislation.[19] Normal restrictions on marketing apply: if someone has required you not to market to them, then this includes marketing by e-mail or other electronic means.

It is quite likely that the e-commerce regulations apply to some aspects of fundraising, including getting people to become members of your organisation, and they certainly would apply to on-line trading from catalogues, etc.

These topics are covered in more detail in Chapter 15.

Practical implications

It is important that, if you make any use of direct marketing, your system is able to record who has consented or objected to what. The system must be reliably able to 'suppress' any individual's details if they have opted out. While a manual system may suffice for small numbers, an automatic system is likely to be more accurate.

It is up to you whether you allow nuances in opting out. There is nothing to prevent you giving people the choice to receive, for example, information about membership benefits but not a trading catalogue, or invitations to participate in sponsored events but not raffle tickets. The basic minimum, however, is a blanket 'yes' or 'no' to all marketing material.

When someone does opt out, deleting them altogether from your database may be unwise. If you ever came across their name again, you would have no record that they had exercised their direct marketing opt-out and you may inadvertently end up marketing to them again, against their wishes.

You must also ensure that if you transfer information to other organisations for marketing purposes, either you exclude anyone who has opted out of direct marketing, or you include their opt-out status with the information transferred. If you obtain information from other organisations you need guarantees that they have excluded (or marked) those who have opted out of direct marketing.

[19] European Directive 2000/31/EC.

Finally, it is important that all your staff and volunteers who may be in contact with Data Subjects understand the full implications of these new rights. There must be a clear procedure for acting on the wishes of anyone who says 'Stop sending me this stuff' or 'Stop phoning me'.

Summary

Who	Can object to	Who to	How	Under
Data Subject	All unsolicited direct marketing from one organisation	Data Controller	'Require in writing'	1998 Data Protection Act
Phone subscriber	Unsolicited telephone marketing from one organisation	Caller	'Notify'	Telecom. 1999 Regulations
Phone subscriber	Unsolicited telephone marketing from any organisation	Telephone Preference Service	Call 0845 070 0707	Telecom. 1999 Regulations
Business fax subscriber	Unsolicited fax marketing from any organisation	Fax Preference Service	Call 0845 070 0702	Telecom. 1999 Regulations

10

Providing the Data Subject with information

Previous chapters have discussed various situations in which the Data Subject needs to be provided with information and, frequently, offered opt-out options.

This chapter:

▶ Draws these situations together

▶ Gives examples of Data Protection statements

For information on Data Protection information statements in the context of e-mails and the Web, see also Chapter 15.

A balance has to be struck between the clear requirement to ensure that a Data Subject has the information they are entitled to, and the danger of overloading people with unhelpful detail. This is particularly true if your initial contact with people is while they are under stress, or if there are other reasons why they may not be capable of taking in the implications of a Data Protection statement.

The rule of thumb is to ask: 'Have we done enough to ensure that the Data Subject is unlikely to get any surprises from our use of the data (including any disclosure we might make to other people) at any stage?'

As described in Chapter 6, there is certain basic information that all Data Subjects must have. You could consider:

■ a standard short statement on your leaflets and forms;
■ a standard paragraph in letters welcoming new members, donors or clients;
■ an occasional short piece in your newsletter;
■ a privacy statement on your website;
■ a notice in your waiting room;
■ a standard piece in any telephone scripts;
■ notices in contracts – of employment, for example.

Note also that the Act says only that the Data Subject should have the information, not that you have to tell them. So if they already know, or if it is obvious, you need do nothing.

> **Do we have to state on our notepaper etc. that we are registered under the Data Protection Act?**
>
> No. There is no point. You are bound by the Act whether you have 'notified' (the new term for registration) or not.

Data Protection statements

When you are inserting a Data Protection statement in any document, the following checklist covers some of the main considerations.

- Say who you are and the purpose(s) for which you want the data.
- Identify possible disclosures to other organisations or transfers abroad.
- Offer an opt-out from disclosure to other organisations if this is appropriate, or explain the circumstances in which disclosure will happen.
- Offer an opt-out from direct marketing, if relevant.
- Indicate any data items on the form that are voluntary.
- Explain explicitly why you need any sensitive data for which you are asking.
- Be 'fair'. Provide as much information as necessary about how you will use the data, including any security measures or self-imposed restrictions that may reassure the Data Subject.

You may decide that, instead of a single Data Protection statement, it is more appropriate to put the relevant information in different places within the document. This is completely acceptable. The test is whether the Data Subject ends up with the right information. You do not even need to refer to the term 'Data Protection', unless you think it will help your Data Subjects.

> **Do I have to tell people that their data is going onto a computer?**
>
> No. This was only relevant when the 1984 Act applied only to computerised records.

Disproportionate effort

You do not have to provide the Data Subject with information if it would involve 'disproportionate effort'. This is almost the only ground on which information may be withheld. (Others include where the information must by law be processed, or under certain exemptions, discussed below.) This does not mean that you can just decide that it would be too much bother. You must be able to justify this.

The following example of a Data Protection statement was issued by the Co-operative Bank plc in a newsletter to existing customers in April 2000.[20] It is an excellent example of how clear, relevant and useful information can be provided within a regular communication, and without going too far into the technicalities of the Act.

Data Protection: extending your rights

The new 1998 Data Protection Act defines your rights as an individual in relation to the information held about you, and how it may be used.

Like any bank, we hold information about our customers – ranging from names and address to the details of regular monthly expenditure.

Of course, the most important way in which we use data is in providing you with the financial service you have requested. But since, in some circumstances, we may pass on information about you, with your consent – for example, to a credit reference agency – it's absolutely essential that you should trust us to act responsibly, and in your interests.

Our undertaking, your rights

We fully accept this responsibility and are happy to give you a firm undertaking that we will keep information about you up-to-date and accurate, and do everything we can to prevent it from being used in any unauthorised or unlawful way.

In addition to our commitment, the new Data Protection Act gives you more extensive rights in relation to the information we hold about you.

If you prefer that we stop using your information for the purpose of advising you about our services, or if you feel that we are using information about you in any way which you believe may cause you (or another person) substantial damage or distress, you can write to us at the address below to request that your records are no longer used in this way.

However, we hope that you trust us to respect your interests and the information we have about you.

We also hope you have found that The Co-operative Bank places a very high value on trust and openness. If you feel you would like to know more about how we are complying with the new Data Protection Act, please write to Customer Care, Delf House, Southway, Skelmersdale, Lancashire, WN8 6NY. If you would like us to send you a copy of the information we hold about you, please write to the same address specifying your account number and enclosing a cheque for £10 payable to 'The Co-operative Bank plc'.

---

[20] Quoted here with permission.

The Act does not define disproportionate effort, but the Information Commissioner has given formal guidance on this. She will take into account factors such as the nature of the data and the cost to the Data Controller in providing the information or the length of time it would take.

Thus, if you acquire details of another voluntary organisation's supporters in order to approach them for money, the effort of making sure that they know who you are and what you are doing, the first time you write, would be minimal. You should therefore tell them (and give them all the information they need about how to exercise their rights – for example to stop you contacting them again).

However, if your contact person in another organisation leaves and says, 'After I've left, talk to Sam if you need anything', you don't really need to go to the trouble of phoning Sam and saying 'By the way, you're now on our database as the contact for this organisation'.

Where you are using information that is already in the public domain, you are much more likely to be able to argue 'disproportionate effort'. Such information might include a list of journalists on your media database, a list of solicitors in a directory, or details of professionals such as doctors or social workers who are connected with your clients.

> **We carry out profiling of potential major donors before we approach them. Do we now have to tell them we're doing this? That would defeat the purpose.**
>
> Here, by definition, you are obtaining the data from a third party. If you are collecting information from the public domain, and provided your intention is to tell the Data Subject eventually, then you can almost certainly justify collecting the information in secret for a reasonable time under 'disproportionate effort'. However, you should be careful to hold the information only for the minimum time necessary before informing the Data Subjects.
>
> You also have to be 'fair' to the Data Subject, comply with the Conditions, and meet the requirements for good quality data. If the information is from private, not public sources, if it is 'sensitive', and if you don't check it carefully, you are much less likely to be compliant with good Data Protection practice.

Remember that if you decide not to tell people you are holding their information, you *must* by law keep a record of your reasons for believing that the effort is disproportionate. A note in your Data Protection policy or a minute of the relevant meeting are likely to be suitable ways of recording this. It is wise to clarify that the decision has been made formally, on behalf of the organisation, not at the whim of an individual.

You can certainly reduce the effort of telling people in many cases. Could you put a notice in your waiting room? You may decide that you don't then need to say anything further in your discussions with clients, service users or visitors. Could you include the information in something you are sending people anyway – a short statement in your newsletter, for example?

You could also make a point of telling people how to find out more if they want to. Prepare a more detailed statement about your activities which is ready for anyone who asks.

> **We have lots of people on our database whose details we first collected long ago, well before the new Data Protection Act came in. Do we have to go back to them all now and tell them we have their data?**
>
> Almost certainly not. If you are still using the data regularly to keep in touch with them, they already know you have their details, and what you are using the data for. If they haven't been in touch, and you got the data from elsewhere, then you may be able to argue 'disproportionate effort'.
>
> However, you would be very wise to check that you are complying with all the other Principles. Is the data still adequate and relevant? Are you keeping it longer than necessary? Have you told them how to exercise their new opt-out rights – for example through a notice in your newsletter?

Data about third parties

A complication may arise where you collect information about a third party (perhaps another family member, a landlord, or someone the Data Subject is in dispute with) at the same time as getting other information from the Data Subject. In some circumstances, particularly if the information is put on computer, the third party may also be a Data Subject. Do they have to be informed of this, and if so, how?

Where you are fairly sure that the third party is happy with the situation, you are likely to want them to know what is happening. For example, if someone is down as the emergency contact for a child in your care or for a staff member, you have an interest in checking that they know this and have agreed. Otherwise they may not be available when you need them. One way to inform them would be to contact them yourself. Alternatively, when you collect the information from the

Data Subject you could perhaps get them to confirm that they have told the person that their name is being put down, and possibly that they have given their consent.

There may be other cases where you don't want the third party to know you have information about them. Normally you have no option but to inform them. However, see 'disproportionate effort' above.

Other subject information exemptions

There are a very few cases where, largely for obvious reasons, the Act says that you do not have to tell the Data Subject about how you are processing their data. For example, if you decide to disclose information to the police in order to help them prevent crime or catch criminals, you do not have to tip off the Data Subject that you have done this. (See also Chapter 13.)

Another set of exemptions applies to regulatory activity, including 'protecting charities against misconduct or mismanagement … protecting the property of charities from loss or misapplication [or] recovery of the property of charities'. Again, if you need to disclose information for these purposes, you do not have to tell the Data Subject if it would 'prejudice the proper discharge' of the activity.

Similar provisions apply in the case of 'securing the health, safety and welfare of persons at work', or where legal professional privilege applies.

These exemptions are not to be used lightly. Usually it is wrong to keep the Data Subject in the dark, but the provisions are there for the rare occasions when they are needed.

Template for an information panel

It is important not to go overboard in providing information. The example overleaf is not intended to be a model to be used in full. Rather it is a template, where all the parts in round brackets '( )' have to be filled in with your own information, while the parts in square brackets '[ ]' are optional, to be used only if they apply.

The words can, of course, be adapted to suit your particular audience.

We/(The Data Controller) will use the information you have provided here [, and other information you may provide us with in the future] for the purpose[s] of (purposes).

[We will not disclose this information to any other person or organisation, except in connection with the above purposes. / We may disclose this information to other [type of] organisations for the purpose of (purpose). If you object to such disclosure, please tick here □.]

[Other information required to make the collection fair.]

[If you do not want us to contact you about other [products/services/projects/events/etc] in future, please tick this box □.]

[We may want to contact you in future by telephone about other [products/services/projects/events/etc]. If you are happy for us to do so, please tick this box □.]

[We may want to contact you in future by fax about other [products/services/projects/events/etc]. If you are happy for us to do so, please tick this box □.]

We may want to contact you in future by e-mail about other [products/services/projects/events/etc]. If you are happy for us to do so, please tick this box □.]

If you have any query about the use we make of your data, please contact (Data Protection Officer).

[With respect to the data about (sensitive areas) we need this because (details).]

This 'signpost' has been introduced by the Information Commissioner to offer a consistent and recognisable way of drawing attention to written Data Protection statements. For more information (and an option to download the image itself) see the Information Commissioner's website. The signpost and its intended uses are also described in a leaflet available from the Commissioner. However, the signpost has not been widely adopted. On the Web there is some concern that it might be confused with the padlock symbol indicating a secure connection.

Summary

- When you provide information to the Data Subject, make sure that it is prominent, easily identified and easily understood.
- Don't provide so much information that people are overwhelmed, but tell them how to get more details if they wish.

- Put appropriate information in appropriate places – your newsletter, forms that people complete, or your website all need a different approach.
- Remember to ensure that you inform people whose data you get from someone else, unless it involves 'disproportionate effort'.

EXAMPLES

(21) Vince runs a training programme. When organisations book people onto courses they obviously have to provide personal data about the participants. Vince thinks about what he does with the data and decides that he is confident that the Data Subjects know enough about what is going on. His organisation's name is prominent on the booking form, and he uses the information only for administering the training course and making sure everyone pays. The names of delegates are put on the computer, so they are personal data, but he decides not to put a Data Protection statement on the form.

However, the next time he runs a course he finds himself routinely printing off a list of participants and faxing it to the course tutor. He also normally puts a copy of the participants' list into the course packs. On reflection he decides that this may still be OK: he's only doing what people might expect; but he wants to be on the safe side. So he does add a short statement to his booking form explaining that the names and organisations, only, of the participants will be disclosed to the tutor in advance and to other participants.

The next development is that instead of marketing future courses to the participants' organisations, Vince decides to identify courses that people might be interested in and write directly to them. Because this is marketing directed to the individual, he now needs to make this clear on the form, and to offer an opt-out box.

He also decides that he needs to be more explicit when he collects information about special needs.

Vince ends up with a statement which says:

Information you provide in connection with our training courses will not be disclosed outside our organisation, except where necessary in order to facilitate the training. All participants are given a list of participants' names and organisations, but no further details.

If you do not want us to contact you in future about other training courses, events or publications, please tick this box ☐.

Information that you choose to give on special needs will be passed to the venue and/or the tutor, if relevant, so that we can make your participation as rewarding as possible. We will not retain the data after the course.

㉒ The Data Protection and confidentiality poster in an advice agency reads:

This agency has a strict policy on confidentiality and we take good care of any information we have about you. If you want to know more, please ask any of our advisers to explain or to give you a leaflet.

㉓ The clause at the bottom of a job application form could read:

All the information I have given here is true. I consent to the use of all this information for considering my application, and understand that:

- *it will be treated confidentially at all times;*
- *if I am successful it will form part of my personnel records;*
- *if I am unsuccessful the information will be destroyed after six months.*

Signed: *Date:*

㉔ Manesh needs to carry out extensive equal opportunities monitoring of a youth training project. His manager suggests that the information collected could also be used to identify potential participants in special projects aimed at particular groups.

Manesh advises the manager that if they do this they cannot rely on the provisions for equalities monitoring, since they may end up using the information to make decisions about individuals. They therefore come up with the following statement for the form.

You do not have to provide any of this information, but if you do it will help us to make sure that you are getting the best help we can give you. We will not pass the information about you to anyone outside the Project, but we will compile statistics to show our funders and other people how we are doing. This form will be kept separate from our other information about you and your progress, and will be destroyed once you leave the Project.

11

Data Subject rights

The 1998 Act introduces important new rights for Data Subjects, as well as strengthening and retaining rights which existed under the 1984 Act. For the first time individuals can actually prevent Data Controllers using their data in certain ways, either by withholding consent or by exercising specific rights.

This chapter:

▶ Presents a summary of the main Data Subject rights. Key ones are dealt with in more detail in separate chapters, as indicated below.

In summary, the Data Subjects' rights include the rights to:

- receive specific information (see Chapters 5 and 10);
- opt out of direct marketing and telephone marketing (see Chapter 9);
- restrict automated decision-making (see below);
- prevent processing that causes harm to the Data Subject (see below);
- apply for Subject Access (see Chapter 12);
- ask the Information Commissioner to make an 'Assessment' of whether an organisation or person is complying with the Act (see Chapter 18).

Automated decision-making

There are new rights in relation to automated decision-making processes, such as:

- credit scoring – if information is fed in and the decision on whether to grant someone credit is made entirely automatically;
- CV assessment – where a CV that is received electronically might be scanned automatically and rejected if the person is 'too old';
- automatically matching people as they pass in front of a CCTV camera against a file of photographs, to identify people who have been barred from the premises.

Since very few voluntary organisations have systems that make completely automatic decisions, these rights are described here only in brief. Voluntary organisations might be able to help their clients to make use of these rights, and so do need to be aware of them.

As a Data Subject you have the right to 'require' a Data Controller, in writing, not to make any decisions about you entirely automatically.

If you have not done this, decisions may be made automatically, but you have the right to know 'as soon as reasonably practicable' that this is happening. You then have the right to ask for the decision to be reconsidered manually within 21 days. You can go to court to enforce these rights if the Data Controller does not comply with them.

In brief, these rules do not apply if:

- the automatic decision is taken in connection with a legal responsibility or a contract involving you; *and*
- the effect of the decision is to grant your request *or* your interests are safeguarded (for example by allowing you to 'make representations').

What this means is that if, for example, you are turned down for credit, or a job, and the decision is made completely automatically, you must be told this and have the right for the decision to be reconsidered. But if you are given the credit you want, you don't have to be told. And if the final decision on whether to shortlist you for the job is checked by a person, you also have no rights to be told or to object.

Processing that harms the Data Subject

The Data Subject has the right to 'require' the Data Controller, in writing, to stop processing their personal data in ways that harm the Data Subject. Harm is defined as 'substantial damage or substantial distress' that is 'unwarranted'.

This right is available only if the Data Controller is relying on the fifth or sixth fair processing conditions in Schedule 2: the official functions and the 'legitimate interests' of the Data Controller (see Conditions for fair processing in Chapter 5). If the processing is in connection with a contract, for example, the Data Subject cannot prevent it.

If the right to stop processing is exercised, the Data Controller must reply in writing within 21 days, either agreeing to stop or saying why they don't think they should. The Data Subject can take the Data Controller to court if they don't think they have complied properly.

Legal remedies

Many Data Protection problems will be resolved directly with the Data Controller or through the intervention of the Information Commissioner. For most Data Subjects court action will be a last resort. This section is therefore a very brief summary.

A Data Subject may use the court to enforce other rights within the Act, such as those described immediately above and the right of Subject Access (see Chapter 12).

Where someone has suffered 'damage' by a contravention of the Act they can take the Data Controller to court for compensation (and may also claim for associated distress).

The court may order the Data Controller to 'rectify, block, erase or destroy' inaccurate data. This applies even if the mistake was made by someone else who provided the data. Alternatively the court may order the Data Controller to add a statement to the record rebutting the inaccuracy. In addition the court may order the Data Controller to notify anyone they have disclosed the inaccurate information to, if this is 'reasonably practicable'.

12

Subject Access

The Data Subject's right to see the information you hold on them is a significant safeguard against information being used wrongly or held inaccurately. It is important to get Subject Access right, because people who make a request are often at odds with the Data Controller already, and any mistakes will only make a bad situation worse.

This chapter looks at:

▶ The process involved in giving Data Subjects access to information

▶ The information the Data Subject has the right to see

▶ The relatively limited exemptions from access

In principle a Data Subject has the right to know *all* the personal data that you hold about them. This is known as the right of Subject Access.

This right existed under the 1984 Act, but historically it has not been much used. Very few voluntary organisations have had experience of handling a Subject Access request. Nevertheless it is an important right, and if you are a Data Controller you need to be fully aware of it. The fact that under the 1998 Act it applies to much manual data as well as computer records may well increase the number of Subject Access requests that are made.

The basic position is that when someone makes a valid Subject Access request you have to:

- tell them whether any of their personal data is being processed by you, or for you by a Data Processor;
- give them a description of the data, why you hold it and who it may be disclosed to;
- supply a copy of all the actual personal data you hold about that Data Subject;
- say where you got the information from, if you know;

- explain the 'logic' involved in any automated decision you make about that Data Subject, unless it is a trade secret.

There are qualifications to some of these provisions, discussed below.

What is a valid Subject Access request?

A Subject Access request must be made in writing; it may be sent by electronic means such as fax or e-mail.

You may, but do not have to, charge a fee of up to £10. There is nothing to stop you having a different fee for different circumstances, or different types of Data Subject. A Subject Access request is not valid until you have received any fee due.

You must be careful to provide the information only to the right person. This means that you may, and probably should, ask for information to verify their identity.

We've had a Subject Access request from the absent parent of a child whose data we hold. Do we have to comply?

Firstly, you should check that the child is not old enough to exercise their own Data Protection rights. These could over-ride any wishes of the parents (see Chapter 7). Then you need to be confident that the parent does have a legal right to act on behalf of the child. Finally, you need to be satisfied that the parent is genuinely acting in the child's interests. If all is in order, you do have to comply.

If the request is made on behalf of the Data Subject by a third party, such as a solicitor or a parent, you must check, not just the Data Subject's identity, but also that the person making the request is both properly authorised to do so and acting in the interests of the Data Subject. In most cases it would be wise to get written evidence of authorisation.

You may also ask for information to help you locate their records. You might, for example, want to ask if they had ever been a client, or a volunteer, or which branch of your organisation they originally dealt with. You can only ask for 'reasonable' information, and even if the Data Subject can't answer your questions, you still have to make a reasonable attempt to find any data you have on them.

Once you have received a valid Subject Access request you must reply 'promptly' and within a maximum of 40 calendar (not working) days.

Sample Subject Access request form

Date received:_____

NAME OF ORGANISATION

Subject Access request (1998 Data Protection Act)

You are entitled to see most of the information we hold about you. If you want to see it, please fill in this form and hand it in to the office, with the £3 fee.

Your name:_____

Your address:_____

A phone number where we can contact you (if you wish):_____

Please tick if you have ever been:

☐ an employee ☐ a client at our main office

☐ a volunteer in our office ☐ a client at our branch office

If you have not ticked any of the above, please tell us of any reason why you think we might have information about you:_____

_____

If we may have known you under a different name, please tell us here:

_____

If we find any information about you, do you want to:

☐ have a look at it at our office ☐ have us send you a copy

If you are only interested in particular information, please say what that is:

_____

I want to see the records you hold on me, and I enclose £3.

Signature:_____

Please note:

- If the address you give above does not match the one in our records, we may have to ask you for additional identification.
- If you are not the Data Subject (the person the information is about), we will need evidence that you are authorised to act for the Subject.
- We will reply as quickly as we can. We aim to reply within three weeks, but we may take up to 40 days. If you have asked for a copy of the information, we will send it to the address you have given above.
- We have information about members of our organisation, staff, volunteers, clients, and people we think might be interested in our work. We don't keep this information once we no longer need it, so if you were in touch with us some time ago we may no longer have any information about you.
- We will show you everything we have about you, except that we may be allowed to hold back information which is also about, or which identifies, someone else.

You may choose to respond to an invalid Subject Access request (for example, one made verbally) if you wish, but you might run the risk of overlooking an important step. It is probably better to insist on a written application in most cases.

You do not have to respond if a Subject Access request is made too soon after an identical or similar request from the same Data Subject. In deciding whether it is too soon, you have to consider the type of data, your purpose(s) in holding it, and how often it changes.

A Subject Access request form

You cannot insist on people using a specific form for making a Subject Access request, but you may feel that having one would help your Data Subjects. If you do, you could consider including sections that ask for:

- the date, so that you can calculate the 40-day response limit;
- the name of the Data Subject (and any previous names);
- an address to which the reply should be sent;
- any information that you need to verify their identity;
- any information that you need to help you find the records;
- your fee;
- a signature;
- evidence of authorisation if the person applying is not the Data Subject.

It may be worth describing on the form the process that you will follow, and stating the time limit or any self-imposed targets for response. You may also want to give general information, for example about the purposes you process personal data for. A sample form is given on page 71.

What information do you have to provide?

In responding to a Subject Access request, you must in principle provide all the personal data you hold about the Data Subject. You must provide a copy of the information in 'permanent form', unless:

- it is not possible; or
- it would involve disproportionate effort; or
- the Data Subject has agreed otherwise.

The information must be 'intelligible' to the Data Subject. This means that you must, for example, explain any codes used.

You must provide the information that you held at the time when the Subject Access request was made, except that you are allowed to make routine changes. For example, if you sell publications, and a customer asks for a copy of their record and, in the meantime, you receive a payment from them, you are allowed to update their record. You can even delete the information altogether *if you would have done it anyway*. For example, you might take people's details in order to send them a brochure, then delete the information once the brochure has been sent. Someone might make a Subject Access request only to find that by the time you responded you legitimately no longer held any information about them at all.

What you certainly *must not do* is tamper with the information to remove parts you would rather the Data Subject didn't see, or do anything to it that you wouldn't have done in the normal course of events.

A Subject Access request applies to *all* the personal data held by the Data Controller to whom the request is made. If your records are scattered around – in various databases, and in different files held by different people – your task will be that much harder when it comes to finding and collating it all in order to respond. Good information management and good Data Protection practice coincide: get your information organised properly and it will be much easier to comply with Subject Access requests and other Data Protection requirements.

Information you do not have to provide

Although in principle you have to show the Data Subject everything (and provide a copy), there are exceptions, including the following:

- You may be able to hold back 'third party' material (see below).
- You do not have to provide any confidential reference you have *sent* (but you may have to show those you have *received*).
- You do not have to provide information used for 'management forecasting or management planning' if this would 'prejudice the conduct' of your business.
- You can hold back details of your intentions in any negotiations if this would ruin your bargaining position.
- Material subject to legal professional privilege (or the equivalent in Scotland) can be held back.
- There are various exemptions relating to examination marks and scripts.

'Third party' information identifies an individual other than the Data Subject. Material qualifies as third party information:

- either if the other person can be identified as the source of the information, or if they are just included in it – as a family member, a witness to an incident, even just a face in the background of a photograph; *and*
- if you have any reason to believe that the Data Subject could identify the other person. For example, in a dispute between neighbours, even an anonymous complaint might come from someone that the Data Subject can easily identify.

However, 'third party' material is not automatically excluded. You do have to provide the information about the other person if:

- that person has given their consent; or
- it is reasonable to go ahead without their consent.

In deciding whether it is reasonable to go ahead without consent, you have to take account of:

- any duty of confidentiality you owe to the other person;
- anything you have done to try to get their consent;
- whether they are able to give consent;
- whether they have refused consent.

Can a manager refuse access to their comments on staff because of the 'third party' rule?

No. It is very unlikely. There is no special exemption from Subject Access for opinions about the Data Subject. Although the manager may be a 'third party', they are acting as an agent of the Data Controller. It is hard to see how a refusal of consent could be 'reasonable' unless they have given the comments in confidence and can claim that a duty of confidentiality applies.

If you have consent, or if it is reasonable to go ahead without consent, then you *must* include the information about the other person in your response to the Subject Access request. You can also choose to include the information even if you don't have to, but you would have to be careful. For example, if the other person was also a Data Subject of yours, you would have to be sure that revealing the information when you didn't have to was 'fair'. You may also owe the third party a duty of confidentiality.

Do we have to show people references when they make a Subject Access request?

You don't have to show them any *confidential* references you have *given*. You may have to show references you have received, unless the referee has withheld consent and is being reasonable. See also Appendix C.

If you are certain that the information is something the Data Subject already knows – such as just the names of family members living in their house – you may be quite happy to release it without seeking consent. In other cases you may well want to check first whether you have any information about them that they would rather the Data Subject didn't see.

Where you regularly obtain information from other people, or where your records are likely to contain information about more than just the Data Subject, you may need to think ahead about whether you want to withhold it or not.

> **Social Services provide us with a lot of information about clients that is marked 'confidential'. Is it OK to withhold this when a client makes a Subject Access request?**
>
> There is no automatic right to withhold information just because it is marked 'confidential'. While Social Services departments do have powers to withhold information in certain cases, these powers to do not extend to information provided by Social Services to another Data Controller. If they really want to restrict access, they should think twice about giving you the information or come up with a convincing argument for you having a duty of confidentiality that would over-ride Data Protection requirements.

One option is to have an 'open files' policy. If people who give you information know in advance that it will be automatically shown to the Data Subject in response to a request, and that they will be identified, you would have good grounds for arguing that it was reasonable to give the information without going back to seek consent. This might be appropriate where the information comes from people who are providing it professionally (such as managers in a personnel system, or care workers in a client records system). They would have little reason to insist on anonymity.

In other cases you may want to assure people that the information they give will be held confidentially. Then you would have good grounds for withholding it from Subject Access, but you still have to try to obtain consent.

1998 Data Protection Act: Subject Access to 'third party' material

NB: This refers only to Subject Access; it doesn't affect disclosure to others.

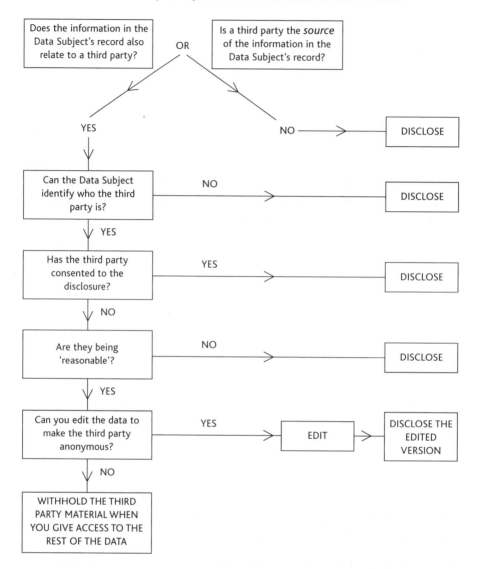

Social work, medical and education exemptions

Parts of social work, medical and education records may be withheld from Subject Access in certain cases which are set out in supplementary Regulations.[21] The Act and Regulations define in detail which records are covered. Normally, records held by voluntary organisations are unlikely to be included. For example the social work exemptions apply to voluntary organisations only if:

- the organisation has been 'designated' by the Secretary of State for Health, *and*
- they are essentially carrying out local authority social work functions.

[21] Statutory Instruments 2000 Nos. 413, 414 and 415.

At the time of writing, the only voluntary organisation 'designated' was NSPCC, and there is no indication that the government is keen to extend the list.

The general ground for withholding information under all these Regulations is that disclosure would 'cause serious harm to the physical or mental health or condition of the Data Subject or another person'. In the case of medical records this has to be assessed by an appropriate medical practitioner. An employer could not, for example, decide for themselves to withhold the results of medical tests carried out on their behalf.

Practical steps

Although you may never have to deal with a Subject Access request, you do need to be prepared. Among other things, you should consider the following steps.

- All your staff and volunteers, particularly those who deal with clients or the public, must be made aware that a Subject Access request has a legal status and that they must promptly pass it on to the appropriate person in the organisation.
- You may want to draw up a Subject Access request form.
- You should ensure when you design information systems that you make it as easy as possible to locate all the information about any particular Data Subject. (See also Appendix E.)
- You have to tell the Data Subject, when you respond, what sort of disclosures you make, and any information you have about the sources of your information. Because of this, you may want to design systems to record your sources and disclosures.
- You may want to consider your policy on withholding information about other people (see above).
- Your trustees or management committee will need to decide your policy on charging for Subject Access.

Above all, because mistakes with Subject Access can have serious consequences, you should consider taking qualified legal advice if you are in any doubt about whether or not you should respond to the request or show specific pieces of information.

Further guidance on several aspects of Subject Access is available on the Information Commissioner's website.

Summary

- Individuals have a right to see most of the data you hold about them.
- You have to reply promptly to a Subject Access request, and within 40 days at most.
- You may charge up to £10 to reply to a Subject Access request.

- You must generally provide, in permanent form, a copy of all the data about the Subject that you held at the time when the Subject Access request was made.
- In certain cases you are allowed to withhold access to information that identifies other people.

EXAMPLES

㉕ Lee is responsible for personnel administration in a medium-sized charity. One of the workers asks to see her file, but Lee is worried because the file contains an old note from her previous line manager that is not wholly complimentary. Suppressing the urge just to 'lose' the note, Lee has to decide whether there are any grounds for withholding it. He eventually concludes that he should not hold it back, since it was not given in confidence, and the line manager wrote it in the course of his work. For the future Lee resolves that personnel files should not contain this type of material in any case.

㉖ A mediation service does not always manage to win the trust of potential clients. Some of them start to make Subject Access requests in order to 'see what people are saying about me'. Linda, the manager, decides on a twofold strategy. Firstly, most of the records will be kept in paper files. Clients who have agreed to work with the service each get their own file, but until then the information is not readily accessible, and therefore not personal data. Secondly, the service will extend its policy on confidentiality, to make it clear that information provided by or related to other people will never be disclosed without their consent.

13

Security and confidentiality

With confidentiality a high priority for many voluntary organisations, security is clearly an important issue. Unauthorised access to information is a big risk, requiring not just written policies, but staff who understand fully how to maintain high levels of confidentiality in their day-to-day work.

This chapter looks at:

▶ The requirements of the Act

▶ Some possible measures to consider

The seventh Data Protection Principle says that a Data Controller must have appropriate security. There are two types of security breach you have to protect against:

■ unauthorised access;

■ data getting damaged, lost or destroyed.

The measures you take must be both technical (locks, passwords, back-ups and so on) and organisational (including training, supervision and management systems).

When a Data Controller has to make a notification (see Chapter 17), this must include a statement about the security measures in place. The Information Commissioner has said that if a Data Controller has implemented BS7799[22] (the British Standard for Information Security Management) this will represent the type of assurance that the Commissioner is looking for. The questions asked on the notification application form reflect the approach taken by BS7799, and you are prompted to confirm that you broadly follow that approach.

BS7799 itself is complex and expensive to implement, and is unlikely to be worth pursuing for most voluntary organisations. This does not mean that security can be ignored, however.

---

[22] Also known as ISO 17799.

What is 'appropriate'?

The security measures you need to take will depend very much on the sensitivity (in its ordinary sense) of the data you process. Your approach should be similar to that in a risk assessment.

- How many people could be harmed by any specific risk?
- How likely is it to happen?
- How great would the damage be if it did?

Information which you could easily replace would obviously not merit such great security as that which would take considerable time and effort to replace, or which may be completely irreplaceable. Highly confidential information would need more protection than that which is already in the public domain.

> **We need highly sensitive health information about the children we take out on trips. What is appropriate security for this? We can't lock it away because then it wouldn't necessarily be available quickly in an emergency.**
>
> Obviously you need to take some precautions. However, all you may need is something as simple as a folder, kept in an unobtrusive place, which you mark clearly with the words 'Confidential: For use by the team leader or their authorised deputy only'. Provided all the other adult leaders on the trip understand that 'confidential' means confidential, this may be sufficient. Other information that has to be generally available must, of course, be kept in a different folder, and possibly in a different place.

Some of your security measures will be general, and aimed at protecting you against disruption as much as anything. Making back-ups and checking incoming electronic material for viruses should be part of everyone's routine procedures. So should making sure that you know who is in the building, and that strangers are not allowed to wander around unsupervised.

You should also take those specific additional measures which protect most effectively against the most serious risks. With confidential client files, for example, you may want to have a procedure for signing them in and out of a secure area, to allow for times when your staff may need to take material out to meetings or case conferences. If you regularly deliver some of your services off the premises – at outreach sessions or in people's homes, for example – this might be a particular concern.

Do I have to buy lockable filing cabinets for all my staff who work from home?

It might be worth considering, but the main thing is to make sure that they know their responsibilities. A lockable cabinet wouldn't help if someone is in the habit of leaving confidential case files on the kitchen table while the neighbours drop in for tea. Provided the person has somewhere suitable to work, which allows them to store papers out of the way of casual visitors, you may decide to put most of your effort into training on confidentiality and security. You should do a risk assessment to help you set your priorities.

If staff or volunteers work from home at all you will need to think about how to ensure that your security measures extend to their laptops (which may get stolen), their home computers (which may be used by other family members), or their kitchen tables, which are all intrinsically insecure areas.

Unauthorised access

From the fact that you have to prevent unauthorised access, it follows that you have to be clear what kinds of access are authorised. This should cover:

- Internal access – who on your staff is allowed access to the information, and for what purpose(s)?
- External access – who outside your organisation is allowed access, and under what circumstances? For example, how do they have to prove their identity, and what methods of disclosing information do you consider secure?
- Exceptions – under what conditions will you breach confidentiality, and who has to authorise it?

Far more security breaches come about through inadvertent, mischievous or deliberate misuse of data by people who are entitled to have it, than by external intrusion. This could mean people looking at files that they know (or should know) they are not allowed to see, or leaving information around where other people can easily read it. Equally you should be concerned to prevent staff giving information over the telephone which should not be given out in this way, and perhaps, in so doing, giving it to people who should not receive it.

The rules should apply equally to permanent staff, volunteers, temporary and sessional staff, management committee members, consultants and any other people who act on your behalf. It is not enough to assume that all these people understand what is meant by confidentiality and security. Your regular receptionist may be quite clear that staff home numbers are not given out; this week's temp may not. Security and confidentiality should be a standard part of the induction for anyone new to your organisation, and should be a regular part of staff briefings, to keep it near the top of everyone's mind.

Individuals who breach security may be committing a criminal offence if they 'knowingly or recklessly' obtain data, or allow other people access to data, without authorisation. It is also an offence to sell data obtained without authorisation. This would certainly apply to stealing personal data for one's own or someone else's use – perhaps copying a mailing list to sell, or going through the files to find information about a specific person. It could even apply to gossip or conversations which allow clients' details to be overheard by someone outside the organisation, or to working on the train where other passengers can overlook, or overhear, confidential information.

This offence can be defended on the grounds that one had the 'reasonable belief' that the action was permissible. This is yet another argument for having a clear policy on confidentiality and an organisational culture that respects it.

When breaches of confidentiality are permissible

Normally, any disclosure must be compatible with the purpose(s) for which you hold data, and must be of a type that the Data Subject is aware of. However, there are two important exemptions:

- where another law requires you to do something, the Data Protection Act permits it;
- where you decide that it is necessary to disclose information in connection with the 'crime and taxation' purposes (see below), there is no breach of Data Protection, provided you meet the relevant conditions.

Therefore if, for example, the Children Act requires you to inform Social Services about suspected child abuse, you must do this without any Data Protection concerns.

It is important to understand that the Data Protection Act does not give anyone (other than the Data Subject) the right to demand information. Their request must be based on a specific other legal power. Many agencies do have the power to demand information, but it is quite reasonable to expect them to know what powers they have. You are therefore within your rights to ask them to produce a warrant, for example, or to specify in writing exactly which powers they are using, and to demonstrate that the person asking is authorised to do so. The request should also be restricted to clearly identifiable individuals. 'Fishing trips' – where they ask for information about a lot of people with no real suspicions – are almost certainly outside the powers of most agencies.

The 'crime and taxation' provisions of the Data Protection Act, equally, do not require you to help the police or customs and excise authorities, for example. They say that if you choose to help them you are not in breach of certain Data Protection Principles. The ones you are allowed to break in making the disclosure are:

- the part of the first Data Protection Principle which says that all processing must be fair (but you must still meet at least one of the conditions for fair processing and the conditions for sensitive data, if applicable);
- the Principles that say you must only use the data for the specified purpose, and that it has to be adequate, relevant, not excessive, accurate, up to date and not held longer than necessary.

Also under this exemption, the Data Subject cannot prevent disclosure under the provision for preventing processing likely to cause damage or distress, and cannot get inaccurate data changed (see Chapter 11).

The 'crime and taxation' purposes are:

- the prevention or detection of crime;
- the apprehension or prosecution of offenders;
- the assessment or collection of any tax or duty.

The exemption can be invoked only if applying the normal rules would be 'likely to prejudice' the purpose.

The Association of Chief Police Officers has agreed a standard form to be used when police are requesting information under the crime and taxation exemptions.[23]

Access control

Our Management Committee feels that they should be able to look at any files they choose to, including confidential client case records. Is this right?

No. They can only look at papers they are authorised to see. And the organisation should be careful, when it authorises access, to respect the second Data Protection Principle which says that all processing must be compatible with the purpose(s) data is held for. If you are offering a confidential service, it is unlikely to be 'compatible' for people to look at the data if there is no operational need for them to do so.

In order to prevent people gaining unauthorised access to information, you may need to consider any or all of the following questions.

---

[23] Section 29(3) of the Act.

- Do your staff members and volunteers know which information they are allowed to see and which not?
- Do your staff and volunteers (including temporary staff and consultants) sign an unambiguous confidentiality pledge?
- Do you require external contractors (such as computer maintenance staff) to give confidentiality undertakings?
- Have your staff and volunteers been trained or briefed on how to keep data secure?
- Are your confidential files in a protected area and/or locked away when not in use?
- Are you careful not to allow unauthorised people to be left on their own in the presence of personal data?
- Do you clear your working area of personal data before leaving the office?
- Are your computers sited so that people cannot see material on the screen that they shouldn't?
- Does your computer system prevent people from leaving personal data on the screen for too long (for example when they leave their desk, or when the next client has already arrived)?
- Do you encrypt or password-protect personal data, especially when you send it by e-mail?
- Is your website isolated from your internal systems and protected from hackers?
- Do you have a system to keep track of personal data that people take out of the office?
- If people are allowed to see some material, but not all of it, do your systems help to enforce this, by storing the information in different places or by requiring a different password for the more sensitive material?
- Do you force people to change passwords and access codes often enough (especially when staff leave)?
- When you deliberately delete material from your computer, do you have the facility to overwrite it to make sure that it is irrecoverable?
- Are confidential manual files shredded or securely disposed of?

Loss or damage

Data in electronic form is particularly vulnerable to loss or damage as a result of computer failure and other technical problems. Manual data must not be overlooked, however. You may need to consider the following questions.

- Are your staff and volunteers aware of all the precautions they need to take? Have they been trained in back-up and other procedures?

- Are irreplaceable documents protected from fire (especially if you ever hold original documents on behalf of service users)?
- Do you avoid taking irreplaceable documents out of the building whenever possible?
- Are your computer systems rigorously and frequently enough backed up, using a recognised procedure? Are back-ups stored off site?
- Do you test your back-ups to ensure they can be restored?
- Do your computer users know how to set their software to make automatic back-ups?
- Do you protect your organisation against computer viruses?
- Do your systems require confirmation before significant material can be deleted?
- Do you give meaningful and consistent names to your files, so that they are less likely to be deleted inadvertently?
- Have you taken adequate precautions to avoid key computers being stolen?
- Do your staff and volunteers take steps to protect computers against damage, especially from liquids or physical damage?
- Do you have a disaster recovery plan?

British Standard 7799

BS7799 identifies 10 key 'controls' for information security.

- Is there a documented security policy?
- Are responsibilities for security processes clearly allocated?
- Are users given adequate security training?
- Are security incidents always reported?
- Is there a virus-checking policy?
- Is there a plan for maintaining business continuity?
- Are legal copyright issues always given due consideration?
- Are important organisational records protected?
- Are personal records processed in accordance with the Data Protection Act?
- Are regular security reviews performed?

These controls provide for the basic level of information security. However, BS7799 also covers measures necessary to achieve a higher level of security, including:

- more on policies and management of security;
- asset classification and control;
- personnel security;
- physical and environmental security;
- computer and network management;
- system access control;
- systems development and maintenance;

- business continuity planning;
- compliance with all relevant laws.

These headings are worth consideration by any organisation which is drawing up its own security policy.

Implementing BS7799 itself is carried out on a commercial basis by the British Standards Institution and other bodies. It involves assessment, advice and audit procedures, and leads to certification which lasts for three years.

Summary

- You must have security measures that are appropriate to the type of personal data you hold and to how it is used. These must prevent unauthorised access as well as inadvertent loss or damage.
- You must describe your security measures when you notify your processing to the Information Commissioner.
- BS7799 covers Information Security Management, but is complex and expensive to implement.

EXAMPLES

27 Malcolm runs a dial-a-ride service. One day, one of the drivers leaves his pick-up list on top of the minibus by mistake and drives off. The details of his clients, including when they will be away from home and information about their disabilities, go floating off for anyone to find.

Malcolm realises that this is a potentially serious security breach. He modifies the minibus dashboard so that there is a recognised place to secure the pick-up lists. He changes procedures so that the lists have to be signed in and out, and briefs all the staff on why he has done this. He reports to the committee, which is satisfied that he has taken 'appropriate' technical and organisational measures both to improve security and to ensure that any future problem is identified as early as possible.

㉘ Most of the volunteers at Sarah's drop-in centre for elderly people come from the local community. One day she overhears two of them exchanging gossip about several of the centre users, which they have picked up in the course of their work. Some of the information is 'sensitive'. Sarah quickly stops them, and realises that many of the volunteers are likely to know users of the centre, or have them as neighbours. In this situation it is particularly important to be responsible about the use of information they acquire about users. Sarah organises a training session for all the volunteers on confidentiality, and strengthens the centre's policy so that volunteers have to sign a statement clearly agreeing not to discuss with each other any information which is in the client files.

㉙ Martha works at a large residential home. A new computer system is introduced for holding residents' details, which includes a lot of 'sensitive' information. The centre manager and shift leaders are trained in how to use it, and given passwords which allow access to all the information, while other workers are allowed to access only basic parts of the record.

One day Martha needs to look up the phone number of a resident's daughter to discuss a change of room with her. When she goes to the computer she finds that the centre manager has been using it, and has been called away urgently, leaving the database open on a very sensitive screen which Martha is normally not able to see. Martha hasn't been told what to do in this situation, or how to close the screen and get back to her normal view of the data. She mentions the incident to her shift leader.

The shift leader's first response is to blame Martha for getting unauthorised access to the data, but Martha manages to convince him that it wasn't her fault. Instead, they compile a report to the information steering group. The group concludes that:

- the centre manager should not have left the screen open; however, since she was called away in a genuine emergency, they decide to take no further action;
- it would be better if the system was redesigned to shut down sensitive screens automatically after a set interval of no activity;
- all staff should be given extra training in what to do if they find the system behaving differently from usual.

14

Transferring personal data abroad

Relatively few voluntary organisations transfer information directly to other organisations abroad. Organisations are more likely, however, to include personal data in information they put on their website. In both these instances, the organisations are transferring personal data abroad under the terms of the Data Protection Act.

This chapter explains:
- ▶ Where restrictions apply to transferring personal data abroad
- ▶ The options that are available to organisations wanting to transfer personal data

The eighth Data Protection Principle imposes restrictions on the transfer of personal data to countries where it is not protected by law. The aim of the Principle is to ensure that Data Subjects do not lose any of their rights when their personal data is transferred abroad. The Principle is modified by Schedule 4 of the Act.

It is important to realise that putting data on a website constitutes an overseas transfer. For more on this, see Chapter 15.

Transferring personal data without further restrictions

For some countries there are no restrictions other than those which would apply to the use of data within the UK. These countries are:

- the countries of the European Economic Area (EEA); and
- those additional countries which have been accepted by the European Commission as having adequate Data Protection legislation.

The EEA comprises the European Union (at the time of writing this includes Austria, Belgium, Denmark, Finland, France, Germany, Greece, Ireland, Italy, Luxembourg, the Netherlands, Portugal, Spain, Sweden and the United Kingdom) plus Iceland, Liechtenstein and Norway.[24]

At the time of writing, the European Commission has announced a decision that, outside the EEA, Hungary and Switzerland have adequate legal protection. It is understood that the law which Canada is introducing in stages will provide acceptable protection in some respects, but it does not apply to voluntary organisations in that country. No decisions have been announced in respect of any of the other dozen or so countries which have Data Protection legislation.

Transferring personal data when restrictions apply

If you are transferring personal data to the vast majority of countries in the world you must take additional steps in order to be compliant. The most likely options are:

- to have the consent of the Data Subject;
- for the processing to be *necessary* in connection with a contract involving the Data Subject, or a contract that is in their interests;
- where you have a contract with the recipient organisation which meets certain requirements;
- where a recipient organisation in the United States has signed up to the 'safe harbors' (*sic*) scheme.

Consent for transfers abroad can be treated in the same way as consent under the Fair Processing Code. It is not safe to assume that Data Subjects will understand the full implications of a transfer abroad. In order to have 'informed' consent, therefore, it would be wise to explain that data transferred abroad will not be protected to the same extent as it is in the UK.

> **We send details of supporters to our partner organisations in India, so that they can send information about their work directly to the supporters. Do we need consent?**
>
> Almost certainly yes, unless you have an approved contract with each partner organisation.

The exemption for information concerning a contract applies only if the transfer is necessary. A clear example of this is travel. If you were sending your staff to a conference in Russia, for example, it would be necessary to provide

---

[24] Note, however, that the Channel Islands and the Isle of Man are *not* in the EEA.

their details to the conference organiser, the hotel, airlines and so on. Whether the contract for these services is with the Data Subject or the Data Controller doesn't matter, provided the contract is in the Data Subject's interests. You must, however, limit the information to what is necessary and, in order to be 'fair', you may want to remind the Data Subjects that they will not have the same control over the use of any data transferred in this way.

> **We send staff to work outside Europe. Do we need consent before we can send details of the staff concerned to our partner organisation?**
>
> Probably not. If the transfer of data is *necessary* for a contract which the Data Subject is party to, or which is in their interests, you do not need consent.

The Information Commissioner argues that it is better to provide adequate protection for personal data rather than to use the consent or contract exemptions, under which the transfer is permitted even though protection may well be lost. A paper on the Information Commissioner's website discusses 'adequacy' in some detail.[25] While it is open to you as a Data Controller to make your own decision on adequacy – or even to decide that the information being transferred is so trivial that it is 'adequate' to have no protection at all – most will prefer to follow the Commissioner's guidance. In the case of countries that have not been approved, this almost certainly means making contractual arrangements with the recipient organisation overseas under which the Data Subject's rights are protected.

> **We recruit volunteers to work with organisations overseas. Do we need consent before we can send their details to the organisation they will be working for?**
>
> You could ask for consent. You probably have it anyway, once you have explained your procedures to the volunteers. Alternatively, you might find that in fact you have a legal contract with the volunteers, or you might be able to enter into an approved contract with the host organisation under which they assume Data Protection responsibilities.

In the past there used to be a problem in deriving terms for the transfer of personal data that the Commissioner could approve. This difficulty was

---

[25] *The Eighth Data Protection Principle and Transborder Data Flows: the Data Protection Commissioner's legal analysis and suggested "good practice approach" to assessing adequacy including consideration of the issue of contractual solutions.* The 'draft' version of this document, dated July 1999, was still on the site in June 2002 and does not appear to have been updated.

removed when the law in England and Wales was amended to permit a contract between two parties to grant rights to a third party.[26] Scotland already had such a provision. Standard terms have been approved by the European Commission, and it is recommended that guidance on these be sought from the Information Commissioner.

Although much relevant material on this topic is available on the Web, it is not possible to give reliable specific references to it. At the time of writing, the documents on the Information Commissioner's website can only be accessed via the index on the 'Guidance and other publications' section of the site. Links to the European Union website are sometimes provided, but do not work if the documents have since been moved.

Special arrangements exist in the case of the United States. During and after the introduction of the European Union Directive, the US made it clear that it did not consider Data Protection to be a suitable subject for legislation, preferring to see it as a contractual matter between the Data Subject and Data Controller. Eventually however, after several years of negotiation, the 'safe harbors' scheme was agreed. Under this voluntary arrangement, US organisations can sign up to a code of practice which guarantees Data Subject rights. Although it got off to a slow start, with only a few large organisations adopting it straight away, the scheme nevertheless provides an approved way of transferring information to the US, and organisations in the UK should be asking their US partners to sign up.

> **We send people abroad to raise funds for us on a 'challenge' which is organised by an external company. What are the Data Protection implications?**
>
> First you need to establish whether the Data Controller is your organisation, with the challenge organiser acting as Data Processor, or whether the challenge organiser is a Data Controller in their own right. This will probably depend on how involved you are in the organising. Whoever is the Data Controller then needs to assess whether the arrangements are subject to one or more contracts (not necessarily ones the Data Subject is party to). If so, any *necessary* transfers do not need consent.

Summary

Transferring information abroad is within the Act if:

- it is going within the European Economic Area;
- the country it is going to has adequate Data Protection provision;
- you have the consent of the Data Subject;

---

[26] The Contracts (Rights of Third Parties) Act 1999, which applies to all contracts entered into after 11 May 2000.

- it is in connection with a contract involving the Data Subject;
- the interests of the Data Subject are protected by an approved contract;
- the recipient organisation in the USA has signed up to 'safe harbors';
- it complies with a limited number of other circumstances.

15

E-mail and the Web

Although there is nothing intrinsically different about applying the Data Protection rules to the use of e-mail and the Web, it is useful to consider in one place the issues affecting electronic communication. Many organisations now feel the need for Acceptable Use Policies or guidance notes on the use of e-mail, and these documents should take account of Data Protection.

This chapter:

▶ Reviews all the Data Protection issues affecting the use of e-mail and the Web

▶ Takes into account the Lawful Business Practice Regulations and the European E-Commerce Directive

Protecting the contents of e-mails

E-mails are in many cases legally equivalent to paper documents. Even ordinary e-mails can be regarded as contractual documents, and a name typed at the bottom of an e-mail is often as good as a signature. Further developments with systems to authenticate e-mails (i.e. to ensure they come from the person they purport to come from and have not been tampered with *en route*) can only hasten this development.[27]

This means that every e-mail must therefore include any information which is required to be given on other documents (such as company and charity registration details).[28] Similarly, as with other documents, e-mails may contain libels or commit the organisation to contractual terms or constitute sexual or other forms of harassment. There have been several well-publicised court cases in which organisations had to pay substantial damages as a result of comments or statements made by employees in e-mails.

If an e-mail includes information about an identifiable living individual, this constitutes personal data and in some cases sensitive data. It is therefore worth

---

[27] See, for example, European Directive 99/93/EC, the Electronic Signatures Directive, implemented in the UK through the Electronic Signatures Regulations 2002, SI 2002 No. 318, which came into force on 8 March 2002.

[28] See *The Voluntary Sector Legal Handbook* for more on this.

taking appropriate security measures to ensure that it does not get into the wrong hands. While mentioning a person by name is not necessarily a problem, transmitting confidential information about a client, for example, would require considerably more care. It should be remembered that, just as with telephone lines, many users, both at home and at work share their e-mail accounts. You cannot necessarily assume that an e-mail sent to a particular address will be read only by the addressee unless you have established with them that this is a secure method of contacting them.

Many organisations try to limit their liability by inserting disclaimers automatically at the bottom of every e-mail sent from their organisation.[29] The consensus among practitioners appears to be that disclaimers at the bottom of an e-mail intended to secure confidentiality (on the lines of 'If you receive this in error, let us know and don't read it') are unlikely to be effective – if for no other reason than that the recipient has read the whole e-mail before they get to the disclaimer. Disclaimers intended to restrict an organisation's liability for the contents (to the effect that the views expressed are those of the sender personally, not the organisation) may be worth considering, provided they are not attached automatically when the organisation does genuinely want to make a commitment.

Instead of using a confidentiality disclaimer, it is better to take specific measures to improve the confidentiality of the contents of e-mails, where necessary. These could include:

- Taking care to establish that an e-mail address is correct, before using it to send confidential materials.
- Enclosing confidential material as an attachment, so that the body of the e-mail can instruct unintended recipients not to read the attachment.
- Better still, using password protection on the attached document, and communicating the password to the recipient through other means.
- Employing user-transparent encryption (i.e. methods that do not impinge on the ordinary user for 'scrambling' the data at one end and 'unscrambling' it at the other) when transferring confidential information between organisations (or parts of organisations) that are regularly in contact with each other.

E-mail addresses

E-mail addresses are regarded as personal data under the Data Protection Act if they are specific to the person concerned, even if the content of the address doesn't identify the individual directly. For example 'johnk453@isp.net' or 'johnk@ourorganisation.org.uk' would be personal data; 'info@ourorganisa-tion.org.uk' would not. (With some addresses, the Data Subject can be

---

[29] It is not the place of this book to give technical details of how to operate e-mail systems. None of the ideas discussed here are technically complicated, and all should be possible using any reasonably recent e-mail software.

identified only from the address and other information the Data Controller holds. These e-mail addresses would not be personal data in relation to a Data Controller who did not have, and was never likely to have, the additional information.) Since a Data Subject does not have to be in the UK, many e-mail addresses of overseas contacts will also be personal data and subject to the Data Protection Act.

Transferring e-mail addresses – those that are personal data – outside the UK is subject to the restrictions in Data Protection Principle 8. If the address is sent to a country without adequate Data Protection, the transfer must meet an appropriate condition. The most likely are:

- Where the transfer is necessary in connection with a contract the Data Subject is party to, or which is in their interests. You could probably use this to require your staff to allow their work e-mail addresses to be used where their work requires them to have contact from overseas. However, a preferable alternative is to use 'generic' addresses wherever possible for general use: 'info@ourorganisation.org.uk' rather than 'smith.j@ourorganisation.org.uk', for example.

- Where the Data Subject has consented to the transfer. Consent must be 'specific, informed and freely given' in the same way as consent as a condition for fair processing.

It is quite likely that if you transfer e-mail addresses by mistake, as a result of poor e-mail practice, you would not meet any of the conditions, and would therefore be in breach of Data Protection. One of the commonest ways for this to happen is where you are sending the same e-mail to a group of people and put all the addresses in the 'To' or 'Cc' fields. Putting the addresses in the 'Bcc' field is usually enough to avoid the disclosure. (However, some users block incoming mail sent as 'blind' copies in an attempt to reduce unsolicited marketing by e-mail.)

For regular mailings, a more secure option is to set up mailing lists on your mail server, so that the sender just mails the message to the particular list and the server takes care of delivering it without disclosing the whole group's addresses to everyone else.

Monitoring staff e-mails

There are many dangers for an organisation if staff misuse e-mails – not just from the Data Protection perspective. Other problems result if careless use results in viruses being allowed in, or if over-use for private purposes starts to have a noticeable impact on the performance of the staff member or the computer system or the organisation's telephone bills.

Many organisations therefore feel the need to monitor staff e-mails, in order to prevent malicious, deliberate or inadvertent misuse. However, monitoring communications in these circumstances is outlawed by the Regulation of Investigatory Powers Act 2000, unless it meets conditions set out in the Lawful Business Practice Regulations.[30] In addition, everyone has a reasonable expectation of privacy under the Human Rights Act. The Lawful Business Practice Regulations, in essence, allow any business — which includes voluntary organisations — to monitor or keep a record of electronic communications (such as phone calls or e-mails) in order to check that no one is misusing the system or doing anything illegal, and for quality control purposes. The main restriction is that you must make 'all reasonable efforts' to inform all users of the system that their communications may be intercepted.

Blanket monitoring and arbitrary intrusion into privacy are not permitted. It is likely to be acceptable to monitor traffic — to note how many e-mails an employee sends or receives, for example — but you must have a good reason to open and read specific e-mails. If you are going to do this, you *must* make the ground rules clear to your staff and, as far as possible, to people from outside communicating with you.

The Information Commissioner recommends that monitoring, where it does take place, should be automated as far as possible, to minimise the amount of intrusion into the contents of e-mails. The implications of all this legislation are discussed in more detail by the Commissioner in the Code of Practice on Employment Records (see Chapter 19).

Acceptable Use Policies

If you decide to have an Acceptable Use Policy it should explain clearly:

- what your organisation regards as acceptable use of e-mail and the Web;
- which breaches will be counted as gross misconduct;
- what monitoring and enforcement action may be taken.

You need to leave as little as possible open to interpretation. Your idea of 'occasional' private use may be very different from someone else's. It is quite usual for every employee and volunteer to be required to sign the policy, and give their consent to the monitoring, before being allowed to use e-mail or the Web.

Heavy-handed monitoring is hard to justify and counter-productive, but if you have an explicit policy, it is easier to take action when you need to. Don't forget that people do have rights to privacy. Reading their e-mails is as much of an intrusion as checking up on how often they go to the lavatory or stare out of the window 'thinking'.

---

[30] SI 2000 No. 2699 The Telecommunications (Lawful Business Practice) (Interception of Communications) Regulations 2000, which came into force on 24 October 2000.

In an Acceptable Use Policy you may wish to:

- Specify how much personal use of e-mail and Web access is allowed, if any. (For example 'You may use the Internet for legitimate work-related purposes only. Personal use is not allowed.' or 'Urgent personal e-mails can be sent, provided this is in your own time and does not interfere with your work.')
- Set out how staff can maintain the privacy of any private e-mails (for example by putting them in a separate folder), while making it clear that total privacy is not possible.
- Ban private use of the e-mail system for commercial purposes or bulk mailings.
- Ban harassment and the sending, forwarding or viewing on the Web, of defamatory or offensive material and make it clear that these could constitute gross misconduct.
- Ban the sending of e-mails in the name of someone else and make it clear that this could constitute gross misconduct.
- Give guidance on the appropriate content and format of work e-mails (including making sure that your organisation is properly identified and that all legally required information is included).
- Give guidance on how to maintain confidentiality, as suggested above.
- Explain that the employer reserves the right to monitor use of e-mail and the Web.
- Set out the circumstances in which monitoring will be undertaken to detect or investigate breaches of the policy, and who may authorise it or carry it out.
- Explain the circumstances in which a person's e-mail will be accessed for business reasons – for example when they are on holiday or absent for other reasons.

Subject Access to e-mails

E-mails sent by a member of staff almost certainly constitute personal data about that staff member (as well as about the person to whom the e-mail is sent, and anyone mentioned in it). This means that you may be required to produce the e-mails in response to a Subject Access request.

The Information Commissioner's guidance note on Subject Access to E-mails[31] states that she would take into account whether the data subject has 'provided sufficient information to the data controller to enable him to locate the data in question'. This means that an 'open-ended' Subject Access request may not be valid. It might well be reasonable for the Data Controller to expect the Data Subject to mention the fact that there may be personal data in e-mails, and to give some idea of the sender(s), recipient(s), dates and/or subjects.

[31] Available on the Commissioner's website under Guidance and other publications: Compliance advice.

The Data Controller, on the other hand, then has to make a reasonable effort to find the e-mails – including looking on the server, on local hard drives, and in any reasonably accessible back-ups.

Collecting personal data on a website

In some ways, information collected over the Internet requires more care, and the Data Subjects require more reassurance, than in more traditional settings. If you are based in the UK, or if any of the personal data is processed in the UK, then UK Data Protection law applies, even if your Data Subjects are on the other side of the world.

Unless your website is merely used for publishing information, and doesn't collect any feedback or information from users (with or without their knowledge), you will need a Data Protection and privacy statement. Some of the information in it will be similar to the information you have to provide on printed material, but other aspects are specific to the Internet. The statement should contain information about:[32]

- Who the data is being collected for (the identity of the Data Controller).
- What personal data is being collected, both overtly and covertly.
- Which of the data being asked for is optional. (Often mandatory fields will be indicated with an asterisk, or shown in a different colour.)
- What purposes the data is being collected for.
- Whether the Data Subject is being asked to consent to use of the data for specific purposes, with provision to indicate that consent.
- Where the data might be transferred or disclosed to (with an option to opt out unless the transfer or disclosure is necessary to the primary purpose).
- What rights the Data Subject has with respect to the data (for example access, correction and deletion) and how they can be exercised.
- How the Data Subject can opt out of receiving marketing material by e-mail (or other means, if applicable).
- How long the data will be kept.
- What security measures are in place, especially where the Data Subject is being asked to part with information, such as credit card details.
- Whether anonymous browsing is possible.
- The site policy on cookies and IP addresses.[33]

---

[32] This section, including the model privacy statement, is based on material written in 1999 by Angus Hamilton, a solicitor whose firm specialises in Data Protection, Internet regulation, computers and the law and litigation, and first published in *PC Pro*. For more information see www.btInternet.com/~hamiltons/. The material is used here with permission.

[33] In other words, whether the website will collect information about the user in ways they may not be aware of. The IP (Internet Protocol) address tells a website how to locate your computer, so that it can send back the Web pages you have asked to view. This information does not necessarily identify you personally but, in some circumstances, it could allow a website to monitor your browsing habits.

- A reminder that linked sites may have different privacy practices (unless you are prepared to vouch for the sites you link to).
- Who should be contacted for more information.

The statement should be:

- positioned prominently;
- linked into all pages that gather data;
- reviewed and updated regularly;
- complied with.

See also the discussion below on using the Web to sell products or raise funds.

Model privacy statement

ABC Ltd doesn't capture and store any personal information about individuals who access this website, except where you voluntarily choose to give us your personal details via e-mail or by enquiring about or ordering any of our services.

In these latter cases, the personal information you give us is used exclusively by ABC for providing you with current and future information about our products and services and any other services described in this website. We don't pass any of your personal data to outside organisations and/or individuals, except with your express consent.

ABC doesn't send cookies from this site and only monitors the IP address of visitors to assess which pages are the most popular. These IP addresses aren't linked to any personal data so that visitors to our site remain anonymous.

You have a right to know about the personal information ABC Ltd holds about you. You also have a right to have your data corrected or deleted. Please address all your requests and/or queries about our Data Protection policy to ABC Ltd at our UK office address.

Publishing information on your website

One of the defining characteristics of the Web is that it is 'world wide'. This means that any information on your site is automatically regarded as being transferred abroad and, by extension, could be going to countries that do not have adequate Data Protection provisions (see Chapter 14).

You therefore have to consider whether you can meet any of the conditions in Schedule 4 which allow you to break Principle 8. In practice, the only one you are normally likely to be able to meet is Data Subject consent.

This means that you should think twice before you put personal data on your website. Remember that personal data in this context includes photographs, because they are being processed automatically, as well as the more obvious written information about the Data Subject. If you do want to publish personal data on your site, you should normally only do so with the consent of the Data Subject.

When seeking consent, in order for it to be 'informed' you probably need to make it clear to the Data Subject that their information is potentially going to countries where it will not have the same level of protection as in the UK.

In a few cases you may decide that you do not need consent. These might include the following:

- Occasionally, you may be able to argue that it is necessary to put the data on your site in connection with a contract involving the Data Subject, or for their benefit, but remember it must be *necessary*, if you want to publish without consent. There are usually likely to be alternative ways of achieving your ends.
- If access to your site is restricted (and your security measures work) you may be able to ensure that the data only goes to people in countries with adequate Data Protection, or who have signed an appropriate contract with you.
- You may decide that where information is already in the public domain (for example the author's name on a book), transferring it abroad without protection is acceptable.

All these situations should be treated with care, however. You may well be in contact with people who are perfectly happy for their details to be available in this country, but who have reasons for not wanting them to be readily available abroad — perhaps in a country they have had to flee as a refugee. Consent is by far the safest route, if you need to put personal data on your website at all.

Using the Internet to sell products or raise funds

The European E-commerce Directive (00/31/EC) was agreed on 8 June 2000 and has now been put into UK law.[34] This covers 'information society services'. These are described, in short, as 'services normally provided for remuneration, at a distance, by means of electronic equipment for the processing and storage of data and at the individual request of a recipient of a service'. It includes services provided free of charge to the recipient (for example funded by advertising) and

---

[34] Under the Electronic Commerce (EC Directive) Regulations 2002 (SI 2002 No. 2013).

on-line direct marketing and advertising. The regulations clearly apply to on-line sales and marketing, whether for products or services, and almost certainly to on-line membership recruitment. It is not clear at the time of writing whether they actually apply to on-line fundraising, but it would be prudent – and good practice – to apply the principles in the regulations to *all* on-line financial transactions.

The parts of the regulations that are most relevant here are those requiring transparency and the provisions for concluding a contract electronically.

Assuming that your organisation is the service provider, you must ensure that you 'make available' to the recipient 'in a form and manner which is easily, directly and permanently accessible', among other things:

- the organisation's name and official address;
- contact details, including an e-mail address, that allow you to be contacted 'rapidly', 'directly' and 'effectively';
- details of your registration in any 'trade or similar register'. This could presumably include charity registration details;
- your VAT number, if applicable.

As well as providing e-mail contact details, it is good practice to provide a phone number so that people have an alternative means of contacting you or checking your bona fides.

'Commercial communications' (essentially, marketing material) must be identified as such, and if unsolicited marketing is sent by e-mail it must be 'clearly and unambiguously identifiable as such as soon as it is received'. This could be taken to mean that the subject line of any marketing e-mail must indicate that it contains marketing material.

Where the whole transaction takes place electronically, you must, among other things:

- make the process clear, comprehensible and unambiguous so that the user knows that they are entering a contract, and knows how to check it and amend the details before confirming the transaction;
- allow them to keep a copy of any terms and conditions;
- acknowledge receipt of any order without undue delay, and by electronic means.

If you fail to comply, a contract will not be valid and you may have to compensate the user.

This is only a brief, provisional résumé of the regulations, prepared as they were being put to Parliament. Further information is available on the Department of Trade and Industry website (www.dti.gov.uk).

There is some debate about where this leaves 'spam' — unsolicited marketing by e-mail. Clearly if someone has opted out of marketing, then you must not approach them in any way, including by e-mail. Some commentators would go further, and argue that unsolicited e-mail is, in effect, outlawed by a combination of European Directives. Others, pointing to the fact that e-mail is regulated by the E-commerce Directive, make the case that you wouldn't need to regulate something if it were illegal.

None of this, of course, can have any effect on spam originating from outside countries not covered by European or equivalent legislation, but for UK-based organisations it is worth being cautious. Many are now adopting an opt-in procedure for e-mail communication. Clearly if someone has consented in advance to being contacted by e-mail there is unlikely to be a problem.

Selling over the Internet (as well as by mail order, for example) is also subject to the European Distance Selling Directive 97/7/EC.[35] This provides, among other things, a cooling off period of seven working days after the order has been taken.

Summary

- You must make sure that your organisation follows good practice in the composition and distribution of e-mails, in order to achieve transparency and confidentiality.
- You should be careful not to disclose e-mail addresses unnecessarily or inadvertently.
- There are limits on the extent to which you can monitor staff e-mails and use of the Internet, especially if you do this without telling them.
- Many organisations find it worth setting out an Acceptable Use Policy for staff access to e-mail and the Web.
- You are very likely to have to produce e-mails sent by or to the Data Subject, or concerning them, in response to a Subject Access request.
- You must ensure that your website provides users with the required information before seeking to collect any information from or about them.
- Publishing personal data on your website (including photographs) almost certainly needs consent.
- On-line marketing, selling and fundraising must take account of the European E-Commerce Directive.
- Unsolicited e-mail marketing (spam) could be illegal.

---

[35] This was put into UK legislation as the Consumer Protection (Distance Selling) Regulations 2000 (SI 2000 No. 2334).

16

Working in collaboration with statutory and other voluntary organisations

Working in collaboration with other organisations often raises complex Data Protection issues.

This chapter considers:

▶ The issues that arise when working in collaboration with other organisations
▶ The problems that may occur when voluntary organisations work alongside statutory bodies which have wider and different legal powers, and often a dominant role in the relationship

Who is the Data Controller?

The first requirement is always to identify the Data Controller. Possible relationships include:

- Each organisation is a separate Data Controller and the organisations merely disclose information to one other. In this case an information-sharing protocol may be useful.
- The organisations are joint Data Controllers. They share the same data, process it for the same purpose(s) and together make the decisions. A charity and a trading company sharing the same marketing database, and using it to promote both the charity's fundraising and the trading company's products, would be likely to be joint Data Controllers. Two or more organisations collaborating to run services for the same client group might be joint Data Controllers. Where there are joint Data Controllers, any

one of them could be liable for any breach of the Act which occurs in relation to the shared set of data. In this case, a contract between the Data Controllers may well be advisable.

- The organisations are Data Controllers in common. They share some of the same data but for different purposes. Each Data Controller decides for itself the purposes it uses the data for, and is responsible for the parts of the data that relate only to its own purposes. This might apply, for example, if a school allowed a parents' association to use its database of parents for regular fundraising contacts and to record the responses. The parents' association would have no access to or responsibility for the school-related part of the database, and the school would not have access to or responsibility for the fundraising section. In this case, an information-sharing protocol would probably be worth having.

- One organisation is the Data Controller with the other being a Data Processor. The Data Processor has no say in the decisions about why or how the information is used. In this case written evidence of the contract is required. This does not always have to be a full-blown formal contract. In some cases an exchange of letters might be enough, but it is in the Data Controller's interests to protect itself contractually from any problems that might arise.

- The consortium itself is an independent Data Controller, disclosing information to and receiving information from its members. Where the consortium is a defined legal entity (such as a company set up for the purpose) this is quite likely. The situation becomes blurred when the consortium is run by a steering group or other body that is partially independent from its members. Legal advice may well be required in such a situation.

Fair processing

If information being collected by one Data Controller will automatically be shared with one or more other Data Controllers, it is essential that the Data Subject be aware of this when the information is obtained. If the sharing is not *necessary* for the purpose in mind, there is an argument that the Data Subject should be allowed to opt out. Certainly, if they do object, there is a danger of not complying with the Fair Processing conditions. The Data Subject has not consented. It could be that the processing is necessary for a contract, or required by law, or falls under the definition of 'functions of a public nature' in Schedule 2(5)(d). But it could be that none of this applies. In that case you would have to argue that the processing was in the legitimate interests of the Data Controller(s) and that it did not prejudice the rights, freedoms or legitimate interests of the Data Subject.

It would also be good practice to ensure that the obligation to inform the Data Subject is recognised by all parties to the consortium. If possible, they should use a common statement or form of words. Only in that way can each of the collaborating organisations be confident that the requirement for transparency has been met and that their processing is fair.

Information-sharing protocols

When it is necessary to clarify in writing the conditions under which data will be shared, and the respective Data Protection responsibilities each member of a consortium undertakes, an information-sharing protocol is often the best solution.[36]

A protocol should set out:

- who it applies to;
- general principles, including the basic principle of confidentiality and a recognition of the different requirements placed on different types of organisation (e.g. the Caldicott regime for NHS organisations);
- the purposes for which information will be shared;
- procedures for sharing information, and in particular for getting and recording prior consent from the Data Subject, and defining the conditions in which disclosure may take place without consent;
- access and security procedures.

Working with statutory bodies

In certain respects, statutory bodies are subject to slightly different Data Protection requirements from voluntary organisations. These differences include:

- The definition of data. 'Accessible records' are those relating to health, education, social work and housing to which access was previously granted under separate legislation. The 1998 Data Protection Act largely consolidates these with general Data Protection provisions, but there are a few remaining differences – for example Subject Access exists to the medical records of people after they have died, even though they are no longer Data Subjects.
- Manual data which will have to be made available[37] under the Freedom of Information Act 2000, and which concerns identifiable individuals, will be treated as data under the Data Protection Act, even if it is not in a 'relevant filing system'.

---

[36] The Information Commissioner has issued specific guidance on the issues raised by information-sharing protocols under the Crime and Disorder Act 1998. Although voluntary organisations do not have specific responsibilities under this Act, many are concerned with its practical application and may therefore be interested in the guidance. A model protocol covering statutory and voluntary organisations can be found at www.idea-infoage.gov.uk/services/dp/index.shtml.

[37] Under provisions currently expected to come into force in January 2005.

- The Fair Processing conditions include the provision for 'functions of a public nature' not to require consent. While a statutory body is almost certain to be covered, voluntary organisations may well not be included, especially in view of the court decision that, for the purposes of the Human Rights Act, the Leonard Cheshire Foundation was not carrying out a public function even when working under contract to a local authority. Voluntary organisations are certainly not given special dispensation in Schedule 3, while many statutory bodies are able to process sensitive data without consent when carrying out their statutory functions.
- Statutory bodies can restrict Subject Access to health, education and social work records, under certain conditions.
- Statutory health and education providers can charge up to £50 for copies of material provided under Subject Access. Voluntary organisations are limited to the £10 maximum.

What this means is that where a voluntary organisation and a statutory one share the same data, they have to be aware that Data Protection requirements may vary according to which Data Controller is under consideration. For example, a file could hypothetically contain some material which would be accessible under a Subject Access request to either Data Controller, some manual information not in a 'relevant filing system' which is only accessible via the statutory body (under Freedom of Information), and some health or similar information which the statutory body can deny access to but the voluntary organisation cannot.

Equally, there may be information which the statutory body can process without consent, but for which the voluntary organisation does need consent.

Wholesale sharing of information may not be in anyone's best interests. It may be better in many cases for each Data Controller to define which information they actually need, and then to restrict the transfer of information just to that information. Since each Data Controller is responsible for its own quality of data, it may even be better to make a referral with minimal data and then collect any other information required afresh from the Data Subject, if this can be done without unnecessary duplication of effort. Alternatively, an organisation could make the minimal referral, then get specific consent for transferring the remainder of the data.

Summary

- Whenever two or more organisations work together, it is important to work out in advance who is, or who are, the Data Controller(s).
- Data Subjects must be made aware of any sharing of data that is likely to take place, and they must be given the chance to opt out if the sharing is not a necessary part of the service.

- It may be worth recording any agreements on sharing, confidentiality and security in an information-sharing protocol.
- Voluntary organisations should be aware that some Data Protection rules apply slightly differently to statutory bodies.

EXAMPLE

③⓪ Half a dozen projects in an inner-city area get together to pool their services. Through a Lottery grant they are able to set up a client database which they all have access to. The idea is that anyone coming into contact with any of the participating organisations only has to go through one registration process. After that they can just turn up to use any of the services.

The Steering Committee for the project realises that there is a complex situation here. Can all the organisations be equally trusted to take good care of the client data? How will the clients feel about their information being shared? They decide that only a clear written policy will do, setting out:

- each organisation's responsibilities as a Data Controller;
- the security measures they will undertake;
- the protocols under which shared data can be used within each organisation.

In addition, the Steering Committee makes sure that the design of the database has strong security precautions built in – for example, so that people can normally see only the basic registration details of each client. If they need to see anything more sensitive they need authorisation, a good reason, and a strictly controlled password.

17

Notification

Some Data Controllers are required to 'notify' the Information Commissioner about their Data Processing activities. For them, it is a criminal offence not to do so.

This chapter looks at:

▶ How to work out whether or not you need to notify the Information Commissioner about your Data Processing activities

▶ The procedure involved in notification

One of the fundamental differences between the new Act and the old one concerns registration, now renamed notification. Under the 1984 Act, the very first question was 'Do we need to register?' If you did, the Act applied to you. If you didn't have to register, that was the end of the story and the Act did not apply.

All that has changed. The first question now is 'Are we a Data Controller?' If you are, all the preceding chapters of this book apply, and your responsibilities under the 1998 Act are considerable. A Data Controller may, in addition, have to 'notify' the Information Commissioner; on the other hand they may not, as there are many exemptions from notification. The key point is that the Data Protection Principles and other provisions of the Act apply regardless. The question of notification is no longer central to everyone who is processing personal data.

However, for those who do have to notify, it does matter. Failing to notify when you should is a 'strict liability' criminal offence: you have no excuse if you get it wrong. 'I did my best' is not enough.

Do you need to notify?

You don't need to notify at all if all your processing of personal data is exempt. The Information Commissioner publishes a useful free booklet, *Notification exemptions: a self-assessment guide.*

> **One of our management committee members was very hot on registration under the 1984 Act. Now that we have decided we do not have to notify under the 1998 Act, he is arguing that Data Protection is none of our concern. Is this right?**
>
> Emphatically not. If you are a Data Controller, then you must comply with the Act, whether or not you are also required to notify.

If you are using the *Self-assessment guide*, you should note that you have to take the questions in order. If you get as far as Question 4 (which lists activities that must be notified) and answer 'yes', then you must notify. Only if you can answer 'no' do you carry on, eventually, to Question 8 where the exemption for non-profit organisations is covered.

The exemptions fall into two main categories.

- Manually held data is completely exempt from notification, under the terms of the Act itself. If you notify a system that is partly held manually and partly on computer, you have to indicate just that there is additional manual material.
- Certain 'core business purposes' have been exempted from notification by Regulation,[38] even if the data is held on computer.

The core business purposes are:

- personnel administration, including payroll, and including volunteers;
- accounts and customer/supplier records;
- marketing, promotion and public relations for your own organisation (which might well, for example, cover a mailing list used to send out annual reports and other general promotional material);
- membership records of non-profit organisations.

> **We are a non-profit organisation. I've been told we do not have to notify.**
>
> There is no blanket exemption for non-profit organisations, although some organisations have reported being given this impression by the staff on the Notification helpline.
>
> An exemption[39] exists for 'establishing or maintaining membership [or] support' or running membership activities. Other activities – such as processing client records, or swapping lists with other organisations – are very likely to require notification if they are carried out on computer.

---

[38] Statutory Instrument 2000 No. 188.
[39] See Statutory Instrument 2000 No. 188.

In each case there are limitations. Generally the Data Subjects, the types of data held, and any disclosures must be restricted to those 'necessary' for the purpose, in order to claim the exemption.

You may voluntarily notify activities that are exempt. The advantage of this is that by notification you 'specify' the purposes for which you are obtaining data. If you don't notify you have to specify the purposes directly to each of your Data Subjects.

Who has to notify?

Notification must be made by the Data Controller. Remember that you cannot be a Data Controller on someone else's behalf. Therefore, each Data Controller has to consider separately whether notification is required. A charity may be exempt while its associated trading company has to notify. A national organisation may need to notify while some of its local branches are exempt but others, perhaps because they keep information on computer rather than manually, also have to notify.

Notification procedure

Notification can be initiated in three ways:

- by phone, to the Information Commissioner – at the time of writing the number is 01625 545740;
- on the Internet – at the time of writing the Web address is www.dpr.gov.uk
- by obtaining a notification form from the Information Commissioner.

In each case you will first have to provide details of the Data Controller. Guidance is available from the Information Commissioner on how to complete these details. For example, in the case of a limited company you have to provide the full company name, not a trading name. An individual has to provide their full name.

In an attempt to simplify the notification process, once you have indicated the general nature of your activities the Information Commissioner can generate a draft notification based on 'typical' activities for that type of business. This will be sent to you (if you phoned up), or can be printed off (if you used the Internet). You make any corrections necessary, sign it, and send it off with the fee.

The bulk of the notification is concerned with the Purposes for which you process data. You are offered a list of standard Purposes to choose from (see box below). For each Purpose that applies to you, you then have to specify your Data Subjects, Data Classes, potential recipients of data and any overseas transfers of personal data.

If the draft you receive from the Information Commissioner does not accurately reflect what you do, you can add or delete Purposes and, within each Purpose, Data Subjects, Data Classes, recipients and overseas transfers. In each case you can make up your own entry if the standard ones really don't apply. You cannot normally use a Purpose twice.

One feature from the 1984 registration scheme which is missing from notification is the need to indicate your sources of information. In addition the standard lists of potential Data Subjects, Data Classes and recipients are significantly shorter. It should therefore be easier to decide whether or not they apply, making completion of the forms both quicker and more accurate.

In the final part of the notification you have to describe in general terms your security measures (see Chapter 13 for more on this), together with various other pieces of additional information.

Notification costs £35 per year for each Data Controller, regardless of how many purposes you have. This means that if any of your purposes at all have to be notified it costs nothing for you voluntarily to add any other purposes for which you process personal data, even if they are exempt. No Data Controller can normally have more than one notification.

If you have decided that you and one or more other organisations are joint Data Controllers for a particular activity, it may well be worth coordinating your notification efforts to ensure consistency.

It may be attractive for national organisations to produce model notification entries, as guidance for local groups. If they do this, it must be made clear that any local group cannot just use the model without checking that it really does reflect their activities.

After notification

Once your notification has been accepted it remains valid for one year. Near the end of that time the Information Commissioner will remind you to renew it.

You have to keep your notification up to date. So if any of the details change, either about the Data Controller or about your activities, you have to ensure that an amendment form is submitted within 28 days. There is no charge for this. Failure to do it is a criminal offence.

You cannot transfer your notification. This means that if you change your legal status (for example, by becoming a limited company or amalgamating with another organisation) the new organisation has to notify from scratch in its own right.

Standard Purposes, Data Subjects and Data Classes for notification

Standard Purposes

Staff administration

Advertising, marketing and public relations

Accounts and records

Accounting and auditing (for other people)

Administration of justice

Administration of membership records

Advertising, marketing and public relations for others

Assessment and collection of taxes and other revenue

Benefits, grants and loans administration

Canvassing political support amongst the electorate

Constituency casework

Consultancy and advisory services

Credit referencing

Crime prevention and prosecution of offenders

Debt administration and factoring

Education

Fundraising

Health administration and services

Information and databank administration

Insurance administration

Journalism and media

Legal services

Licensing and registration

Pastoral care

Pensions administration

Policing

Private investigation

Processing for not-for-profit organisations (membership & related services)

Property management

Provision of financial services and advice

Realising the objectives of a charitable organisation or voluntary body

Research

Trading/sharing in personal information

In nearly all cases the Information Commissioner goes on to expand on what each of these purposes is expected to cover.

Data Subjects

S100   Staff, including volunteers, agents, temporary and casual workers
S101   Customers and clients
S102   Suppliers
S103   Members or supporters
S104   Complainants, correspondents and enquirers
S105   Relatives, guardians and associates of the Data Subject
S106   Advisers, consultants and other professional experts
S107   Patients
S108   Students and pupils
S109   Offenders and suspected offenders

Data Classes

C200   Personal details
C201   Family, lifestyle and social circumstances
C202   Education and training details
C203   Employment details
C204   Financial details
C205   Goods or services provided
C206   Racial or ethnic origin
C207   Political opinions
C208   Religious or other beliefs of a similar nature
C209   Trade union membership
C210   Physical or mental health or condition
C211   Sexual life
C212   Offences (including alleged offences)
C213   Criminal proceedings, outcomes and sentences

Summary

- Any Data Controller may, potentially, have to notify the Information Commissioner about their Data Protection activities.
- Notification can be initiated by telephone or on the notification website, where further guidance is available, or by requesting an application form.
- The annual fee is £35, regardless of the size or complexity of the activities being notified.
- Certain activities (including all manual processing) are exempt from notification. However, this does not exempt them from any other aspect of the Act.
- Exempt activities may be notified voluntarily.
- Failure to notify when it is required is a criminal offence.

18

Enforcement, offences and penalties

The Information Commissioner has not, as yet, made much use of her legal powers, preferring to promote good practice through publicity and example. However, the Act gives the Commissioner important powers.

This chapter summarises:

▶ The powers of the Information Commissioner

The Data Protection Act is enforced by the Information Commissioner, who also has responsibility (in England and Wales) for enforcing freedom of information and the Telecommunications (Data Protection and Privacy) Regulations 1999. The Commissioner's Office is an independent regulatory authority, reporting directly to Parliament.

The first Data Protection Registrar, from 1985, was Eric Howe. His successor was Elizabeth France, who briefly became Data Protection Commissioner under the 1998 Act, then Information Commissioner when freedom of information was added to her responsibilities. It has been announced that her term of office will finish in November 2002, when Richard Thomas will take over the post.

The Commissioner does not have a large staff – around 150 – and is funded by income from notification fees and other charges, not by government grant.

The 1998 Act has considerably strengthened the enforcement powers of the Commissioner, and her staff for the first time have powers of entry and inspection when they are investigating breaches of the Act.

Codes of practice

An important new provision in the 1998 Act is that the Information Commissioner now has both a power and a duty to promote good practice. In particular she can endorse Codes of Practice for particular types of activity or industry sectors. If she believes a Code of Practice is necessary and the industry has not produced one, she can even impose one of her own.

Failure to adhere to a Code of Practice could be viewed adversely by the courts. They must, therefore, be legally watertight and the process of producing them is lengthy. At the time of writing the Commissioner had issued one on closed circuit television (CCTV) and was in the process of releasing a much delayed Code of Practice on employment records. This was being brought out in four parts of which only the first, covering recruitment and selection, had been issued at the time of writing (see Chapter 19).

It is understood that further Codes of Practice under consideration include one aimed at small businesses and one on marketing. Both might be relevant in part to voluntary organisations, but their appearance was certainly not imminent at the time of writing. It is very unlikely that the Commissioner will draw up any Codes of Practice specifically dealing with the voluntary sector, nor will she be keen to consider endorsing Codes drawn up by the voluntary sector itself; reviewing them and agreeing amendments would take almost as much effort as drafting them internally.

What appears more likely is that the Commissioner may offer limited endorsement and encouragement to guidance notes produced by the voluntary sector, dealing with specific issues. This could, of course, change under the new Commissioner, who is due to take up office before the end of 2002.

Notification

Notification is one aspect of enforcement. Processing without having notified when you should have done so is an offence. This is a 'strict liability' offence: you cannot argue that you did your best. It is also an offence not to keep your notification up to date. On this you *can* argue that you exercised 'due diligence'.

Assessments

Anyone may ask the Information Commissioner to make an Assessment as to whether a Data Controller appears to be complying with the Act. The person making the request must believe themselves to be directly affected by the processing they want assessed. The Commissioner *must* then make an Assessment, provided she has enough information to identify the person making the request and the processing in question.

The Commissioner can choose how to make the Assessment. She can specifically take into account:

- whether the request raises a matter of substance;
- any undue delay in making the request;
- whether the person is entitled to make a Subject Access request.

What this appears to mean is that requests for Assessment should not be used when the matter could have been resolved directly with the Data Controller or through a Subject Access request. If the Commissioner thinks this is the case, it may affect how the Assessment is carried out.

The Commissioner has to tell the person making the request whether she has made an Assessment, and may – but is not obliged to – tell them the outcome.

An Assessment is only the Commissioner's opinion, but would obviously carry some weight if the matter later came to court.

Information notices

The Commissioner may issue a Data Controller with an Information Notice, either as part of an Assessment or for reasons of her own. This will ask the Data Controller to provide specific information within a specified time limit, with the aim of enabling the Commissioner to decide whether the Data Protection Principles are being complied with.

Failure to comply with an Information Notice is an offence, unless the Data Controller can show that they 'exercised due diligence' to comply. The Data Controller can appeal against an Information Notice to the Information Tribunal.

Enforcement notices

Where the Commissioner is satisfied that the Act has been contravened she can issue an Enforcement Notice, telling the Data Controller what they must do in order to bring their activities into line.

Failure to comply with an Enforcement Notice is an offence, unless the Data Controller can show that they 'exercised due diligence' to comply. The Data Controller can appeal against an Enforcement Notice to the Information Tribunal.

Powers of entry

The Commissioner can apply for a warrant from a circuit judge to enter and inspect premises if she has reasonable grounds for suspecting that an offence under the Act has been committed or the Data Protection Principles are being broken.

The warrant may be granted only if the Information Commissioner has tried to get access by agreement and been refused, unless the judge is convinced that giving advance warning would defeat the object.

It is a criminal offence to obstruct a warrant, with a maximum fine of £5,000.

Individual offences

In addition to the offence of obstructing a warrant, individuals commit an offence if they 'knowingly or recklessly' obtain or disclose personal data without authorisation from the Data Controller. Possible defences include having the 'reasonable belief' that what they did was permissible.

If a person has obtained data they are not entitled to, it is a further offence to sell it or offer to sell it.

It may be worth making staff, volunteers and trustees / management committee members who have access to personal data aware of these provisions.

Penalties

All offences under the Act, except obstructing a warrant, can be tried either in the Magistrate's Court or the Crown Court. The maximum penalty is a fine of £5,000 in the Magistrate's Court or an unlimited fine in the Crown Court.

Who gets taken to court, should it come to that, depends on the offence. Where the offence is an individual one, it is obviously the individual who would be charged. Where the organisation has committed an offence to do with notification or not cooperating with the Commissioner, the organisation would be charged. However, an unincorporated association (see Appendix A) *cannot* be taken to court in its own right. In this case it would most likely be all the members of the board or management committee who would end up being personally charged.

If your organisation is incorporated, the directors or senior officers may also be *personally liable* if they consented to or connived at the offence, or if they were negligent.

Summary

The 1998 Data Protection Act is enforced by the Information Commissioner.

The Commissioner can:

- produce, endorse and promote Codes of Practice;
- make an Assessment;
- issue an Information Notice;

- issue an Enforcement Notice;
- apply for a warrant to enter and inspect premises.

Failure to notify and failure to keep a notification up to date are offences.

Individuals commit an offence if they knowingly or recklessly get access to data without permission or permit someone else to have unauthorised access, and a second offence if they then try to sell it.

The maximum penalty for any offence is £5,000 if tried in the Magistrate's Court, but most can also be tried in the Crown Court, with unlimited fines.

19

Taking stock: Data Protection audits and policy development

There are so many strands to Data Protection that it is often difficult to know where to begin. For many organisations, the first step is to identify gaps in their systems and then take action to fill them.

This chapter:

▶ Describes an approach based on the Information Commissioner's recommendations on Data Protection auditing

▶ Looks at how to draw up appropriate policies

▶ Offers advice on where guidance may be found, including the Commissioner's Codes of Practice.

The Information Commissioner recommends carrying out a Data Protection audit, and has produced guidance on her website and on a free CD-ROM. The Commissioner's scheme is exhaustive, and probably too elaborate for many small voluntary organisations. However, the general approach has much to recommend it. The process is split into two parts: an 'adequacy' audit, and a 'compliance' audit. In essence the adequacy audit asks 'Has the organisation identified its processing of personal data, made the necessary decisions and produced the necessary policies?' The compliance audit then looks at whether the policies are being followed and the Data Protection Principles complied with.

As with any audit, it is possible to carry out the procedure internally, using your own staff, or externally, for greater objectivity (but, inevitably, at much greater cost). Your choice on whether to buy in support may partly depend on whether you have the necessary expertise in house. The Commissioner recommends that the adequacy part of the audit is best done externally.

The adequacy audit

An adequacy audit is largely a desk exercise. It is supposed to check that existing policies comply with Data Protection requirements. Inevitably, however, many organisations will already be aware that they have work to do in some areas. If you are in this situation, it may be a more economical use of time to combine the auditing process with the remedy: where policies do not exist, they can be drawn up, using the impetus of the audit.

The audit may also throw up specific tasks that need to be undertaken: many organisations find that they need to work out who all their Data Processors are, and systematically review their contracts.

In other cases legal advice may be required to answer apparently simple questions such as 'who is the Data Controller?' before you can decide who is responsible for drawing up policies.

Finally, the audit should identify lines of accountability and responsibility within the organisation, from the board of trustees or management committee to those staff or volunteers who actually handle the personal data.

Identifying relevant policies is not always easy. Typically, they will be scattered in a number of places, such as staff handbooks, confidentiality policies, or fundraising guidelines. It is often useful to start by thinking about key types of Data Subject – clients, personnel, and so on – then to ask the relevant staff and volunteers what written policies they have produced or are aware of.

Almost inevitably you will realise that the policies you find do not cover all aspects of Data Protection, and may even be inconsistent with each other. It will probably be necessary to draft additional material or amend existing documents, and to prepare a summary showing how all the different documents relate to each other.

Subsequently, adequacy audits should be much more straightforward, as they will be able to review a complete set of documentation.

Policies

Many organisations ask for model Data Protection policies. But good Data Protection practice is based on the Data Protection Principles, not rules, and the Principles have to be applied according to the particular circumstances of each organisation. Because of this, it is hard to offer examples without making them so general that you may as well start from scratch.

It is possible, however, to suggest a process.

1   You should begin by identifying your key Data Subjects. These will typically include clients, personnel (paid and/or volunteer), members, donors and supporters, and a wide range of professionals and contacts in your field.

2   You should then identify key areas of concern for each type of Data Subject. With clients, the main issue might be confidentiality and disclosures (for example, disclosures you have to make to other agencies or funders). For donors, the issue may centre on the marketing opt-out. Staff may be most concerned with Subject Access, especially for specific parts of their record, such as references.

3   Now you need to identify decisions which have been made about these and other relevant issues – or, if necessary, make the decisions. With personnel files, for example, do staff have an automatic right of access to their own file, regardless of Data Protection? How much, if anything, do you charge for Subject Access, and does it vary with circumstances? How long do you retain different types of record? Under what circumstances would you reveal confidential information, and who has to authorise this? If the information is sensitive you need to be especially clear which of the Schedule 3 condition(s) you will be able to meet.

4   Above all, you need to know how you comply with the transparency requirements. What do you need to tell people, and when and how is this done? If you are going to use the 'disproportionate effort' exemption to avoid telling people when you have obtained their data from third parties, why do you think it applies and where is it documented?

5   It is usually then possible to add in uncontroversial points from other Data Protection Principles. You need to be clear why you hold the information on each Data Subject, including any secondary uses you make of it, and you should remind everyone about the requirements for data to be adequate, relevant, not excessive, accurate and up to date.

Your written policy should set out the standards you aim to meet, in terms that the Data Subject can easily understand. Do not be tempted to write too much. A short, clear policy is likely to be far more effective than a detailed one that no one uses. The details of how you will achieve the standards should be set out in any procedures you then develop. See the example on page 122.

Example[40]

An agency has the following statement prominently displayed in its waiting room:

> 'Nothing you tell us leaves the agency without your consent except in rare instances. If you would like to know more about what happens to the information we collect, please ask for a leaflet.'

The leaflet is made up of two sides of A5. One side says:

> 'You will already be aware that whilst you have been talking to someone here, that person has been writing down some notes about you.
>
> It is important to let you know how we use that information and how we ensure that it cannot be misused in any way.
>
> We will not normally use your data in a way you would not wish. This includes keeping any information you give us about yourself confidential at all times except in very specific circumstances (see the reverse side of this page).
>
> The reason we take information about you, in the first instance, is so that the person you are seeing can read back over this information and think how best to support you, which may involve sharing some information with appropriate colleagues. You can take a copy of this information away with you if you wish.
>
> The other reason we keep your information is for statistical purposes, so that we can make sure we are providing the right kind of service for as many people as possible. We also give some of the statistical data to the people who fund us, but we must make it clear that no one can be identified through this data (for example, we tell our funders how many males and females have contacted us – obviously completely anonymously).
>
> If you have any specific questions about how we use your information or look after it, please ask the person you are seeing or our other advisers to put you in touch with_____.
>
> Additionally, if you have any suggestions for us on how we can give you a better service, please let us know.'

---

[40] This example is used with permission.It has been sligthlty edited to avoid identifying the source.

The other side of the leaflet says:

> **'Confidentiality**
>
> Any information that you give about yourself when you are here is confidential to the agency and will not be given out to anyone without your express permission.
>
> You should be aware that there are four occasions when we have no choice about what remains confidential. They are:
>
> - If there is a real concern that you are putting a third person at risk e.g. suspected child abuse.
> - Where we are instructed to do so by the Social Services Department under specific legislation.
> - When we are required to do so under the Prevention of Terrorism Act 1989, the Drug Trafficking Offences Act 1986, other legislation requiring disclosure or during an investigation by the Serious Fraud Squad.
> - Should you fall seriously ill while you are here and we have to give information to medical personnel.'

The compliance audit

Once you have a policy statement, there is something to measure your Data Protection performance against. To do this thoroughly can be time consuming; again it is worth setting priorities so that you devote your energy to the issues likely to be threats, either to your own activities or to the interests of your Data Subjects. You may find that some areas of your policy are almost self-policing: with personnel records, for example, it is quite likely that any major problems would come to your attention by other means. A 'light touch' compliance audit may just consist of an annual interview with the personnel officer to go over their procedures and perhaps a questionnaire to staff and volunteers from time to time to allow them to raise any concerns.

With clients or members, however, you are likely to have to be more formal and systematic. You should:

- examine all the relevant documents, including forms, brochures, standard letters, Web pages and so on, to ensure that your statements are clear, accurate and consistent, and that relevant opt-outs are offered;
- go through any written procedures to check that they pay due attention to Data Protection;
- look at the recording system to make sure it is structured so as to hold the relevant information;

- review a sample of records (paying due attention to confidentiality) to spot any possible problems with data quality, retention periods and so on;
- interview relevant staff to check that their daily practice is based on an understanding of the policy and any written procedures.

Procedures and guidance on good practice

As time goes on, it is inevitable that guidance on procedures and good practice will emerge. At the time of writing, however, very little is available. Few national organisations or umbrella bodies have yet produced practical guidance; it is to be hoped that this situation gradually changes. In the meanwhile, it is worth asking any such organisations that are relevant to your area of work whether they have produced anything; where they have, your work may be considerably simplified. A network, federation or national body could get involved in:

- producing clear standards that members are expected to follow;
- drafting sample statements, policies and procedures;
- identifying centres of excellence that other members can learn from;
- offering advice on Data Protection;
- providing advice on the design of manual or computer information recording systems.

In a few areas, the Information Commissioner has produced Codes of Practice which do offer guidance.[41] These are not definitive statements on the law. However, they do carry legal weight as official recommendations as to how the legal requirements can be met. If you do not follow a Code, you must be able to show how your alternative solution complies with the Act, and you may have to justify your approach if the Commissioner takes enforcement action. One of the first Codes covered Closed Circuit Television (CCTV) surveillance schemes. Among the points of interest are:

- The equipment should be sited in such a way that it only monitors those spaces which are intended to be covered by the equipment.
- In order to achieve transparency, there should be clear signs so that the public is aware that they are entering a zone which is covered by surveillance equipment, and the signs should state who is responsible for the scheme, its purposes and who to contact for more information.
- Covert monitoring is only allowed in limited cases for crime prevention.
- The images must be of good enough quality to achieve their purpose(s).
- The images must not be kept longer than necessary.
- Access to the images should be restricted to staff who need to see them and understand the implications of confidentiality.
- Subject Access raises particular issues because of the likelihood of there being third party material in the images.

---

[41] Available on the Commissioner's website, under Guidance and other publications: Codes of practice.

Of more interest to most voluntary organisations is likely to be the Code of Practice on employment records. This was much delayed. A draft appeared in October 2000, but the consultation and revision period on the final version was repeatedly extended, and it was eventually announced that it would come out in four parts. At the time of writing only the first part, covering Recruitment and Selection, had appeared in its final form. Part 2 covers Records management, Part 3 deals with Monitoring at work, and Part 4 concerns Medical information. Voluntary organisations should note that the Code does not specifically address any questions concerning volunteers, as opposed to paid staff, although many of the recommendations will be equally applicable.

The Code is lengthy and detailed, but it is worth looking at the standards it recommends. The areas covered in Part 1 include: Advertising, Applications, Verification, Short-listing, Interviews, Vetting (including notes on the Criminal Records Bureau) and Retention of records. Part 1 also looks at the circumstances in which sensitive personal data may legitimately be used during recruitment and selection.

In the absence of guidance, the areas you are most likely to have to consider in reviewing your practices include:

- making sure that Data Subjects have all the information they are entitled to;
- offering clear opt-outs at all relevant times;
- making sure that your internal procedures respect opt-outs, and comply with any assurances given at the time information was collected (such as the purposes you have specified);
- reviewing the Data Protection implications whenever you think about using information for any new or even slightly different purpose;
- making sure that you meet the fair processing conditions and, if necessary, the additional conditions for sensitive data;
- having a clear policy on disclosures, and security systems to support this;
- having effective procedures for handling Subject Access.

Summary

- An 'adequacy audit' involves checking that you have the right policies in place.
- A 'compliance audit' involves checking that these policies are complied with.
- These audits can be carried out by your own staff, but a small amount of external input is often advisable.
- Although you will want to avoid unnecessary paperwork, key policies and decisions must be documented.
- Where the Information Commissioner has produced a Code of Practice, it is advisable to be aware of the standards it recommends and to follow them where applicable.

20

Training your staff and encouraging good Data Protection practice

This topic deserves a chapter of its own, because it is the key to Data Protection compliance. You can understand the Act, draw up policies, and design systems that guide people towards compliance, but if your staff and volunteers don't understand what to do, and how to do it effectively, none of this effort will have the desired effect.

This chapter:

▶ Suggests a training strategy and includes a suggested basic briefing on the Act

▶ Looks at where Data Protection responsibility might be located within your organisation

Staff and volunteers are your biggest security risk where Data Protection is concerned. Problems can, of course, arise from external intrusion or from deliberate unauthorised access. But far more often, it is people who are authorised to have access, but are then careless or unwitting in the way they use the information, who cause trouble.

The key to effective training in this area is 'little and often'. By reminding people regularly of their responsibilities, not only do you keep them alert, you also build Data Protection into the culture of your organisation. Instead of issuing memos and lengthy written guidance, or relying on people's induction training – when Data Protection will be one of hundreds of topics they have to absorb – it is probably more effective to spend 15 minutes at a quarterly staff meeting giving your team a case study and discussing the correct course of action.

Your training programme may look something like this:

- A briefing for your board of trustees or management committee and senior management team, outlining their main responsibilities. This may need to be repeated every two or three years.
- Training for a small number of staff – or just one, depending on the size of your organisation – who will have Data Protection responsibilities in their job description. They will then be able to work on any audits, policies or procedures you need.
- Incorporation of basic Data Protection into your induction programme for new staff and volunteers, especially covering confidentiality.
- Initial basic Data Protection training for all your existing staff and volunteers.
- Preparation of simple guidelines that people can refer to in specific, rare situations – for example what to do if a Data Subject makes a Subject Access request, what to do if the police or another official agency asks for information.
- Regular inclusion of case studies and snippets of Data Protection good practice in team meetings.

You should encourage staff to consider the Data Protection aspects of all new projects and activities. For example, there are bound to be implications if you embark on a new collaborative activity, if you set up a website, or if you outsource a piece of work to a new Data Processor. It should be one of the items that must be checked off before authorisation is given to go ahead.

When you carry out staff monitoring, supervision and appraisal, you should pay attention to any Data Protection responsibilities the person has.

Briefing documents

One of the difficulties with Data Protection is that it is hard to understand individual elements in isolation. You often need the whole picture, or certainly a large part of it. The following sample briefing sheet is not intended to answer all the questions, but to provide a context in which you can go on to point out in more detail the specific implications for your organisation. You may wish to use something like this (with local adaptations) in briefing your management committee or board and those staff and volunteers who just need the minimum introduction to the Act.

When you HOLD personal data

- You are allowed to use it only for the purpose(s) for which it was originally obtained.
- You have to take good care of it. (Security must be 'appropriate'.)
- You have to use it 'fairly'.
- You must ensure that it is: adequate, relevant, not excessive, accurate, up to date if necessary, and not held longer than necessary.
- You are committing an offence if you get access to personal data you are not authorised to, or if you disclose it to people you are not supposed to 'knowingly or recklessly'.

When you OBTAIN personal data

- You have be transparent. This means making sure that the person from whom you are getting the data knows which organisation is collecting the data, and why and how the data will be used.
- You must not deceive or mislead anyone.
- If you get the data from someone other than the individual themselves (the 'Data Subject'), you have to make sure that the Data Subject knows as soon as practicable who is using their data and why and how it will be used.
- You may have to get consent from the Data Subject to use their data, particularly if it is in any of the 'sensitive' categories. ('Sensitive' data covers the Data Subject's racial or ethnic origin, religious or political beliefs, Trade Union membership, health, sex life or criminal record.)
- You may also have to offer them the chance to opt out of some uses of the data, such as direct marketing, disclosure to other organisations, or use for secondary purposes.

When you DISCLOSE personal data

- You have to check that the disclosure fits the purpose or purposes for which the data is being held.
- You have to check that the person you are disclosing it to is authorised to have it.
- You have to check that the Data Subject is aware that this type of disclosure is possible, or that there is an over-riding reason (such as a legal obligation).
- If you put personal data onto the Web, you nearly always need consent from the Data Subject.
- If you transfer data outside the European Economic Area (EU plus Iceland, Liechtenstein and Norway) special rules might apply.

Data Subjects have new RIGHTS

- Where you need a person's consent, you can't use the data if they don't give consent (but you can explain the consequences of not giving it).
- You cannot use data for direct marketing of any goods or services if the Data Subject has told you not to.
- If you are phoning people at home for direct marketing, you have to check that the number you are calling is not on a barred register and these are restrictions on marketing by fax or e-mail.
- Data Subjects can ask to see virtually all the personal data you hold on them, including manual files. The organisation has 40 days to comply with the request and can charge up to £10.

Allocating responsibility

Although your board or management committee has ultimate responsibility and Data Protection must also be a concern of the senior management team, most organisations find that they need to identify a member of staff who takes a lead on Data Protection on a day-to-day basis. In small organisations there may be little choice as to who takes on this role. Larger organisations, however, often find it hard to work out the best place to locate their Data Protection compliance role.

Options include:

- **The legal department**
  This has the benefit of putting Data Protection on the same footing as a range of other legal matters, but it may be somewhat remote from day-to-day operations.
- **Internal audit or quality standards**
  The advantage of putting Data Protection here is that the activities giving rise to the most serious Data Protection concerns are likely to be covered.
- **Information services**
  Because there are substantial elements of information management in Data Protection, it may be appropriate to use people with these specific skills as a central resource for the organisation.
- **Fundraising or public relations**
  Good Data Protection practice can enhance an organisation's image and help to build trust with those outside.
- **Trading or customer services**
  For some organisations most Data Protection issues are likely to arise between the organisation and customers or service users, especially over marketing opt-outs.

- **Human resources**
  If an organisation has relatively little contact with individuals outside, most of the Data Protection questions that arise may be to do with staff records.
- **Information technology**
  In the past it was common to make the IT manager responsible for Data Protection, because it applied only to data held on computer. Now that Data Protection extends to manual records as well, this is less appropriate. The IT department does still need to be involved, however.

Summary

- You must brief your board of trustees or management committee on their responsibilities.
- Training your paid staff and volunteers is more important for Data Protection compliance than large amounts of paperwork.
- Initial induction training should be topped up regularly with brief reminders.
- Guidance notes should be short and to the point.
- It is not always easy to decide where in your organisation the ultimate responsibility for day-to-day Data Protection compliance should lie, but it is important to locate it somewhere.

Further information

It is the Information Commissioner's intention to produce written guidance on various aspects of the Act, in response both to demand from enquirers and to her own priorities. The most useful source of further information is therefore the Commissioner.

Information Commissioner
Wycliffe House
Water Lane
Wilmslow
Cheshire
SK9 5AF
Switchboard: 01625 545700   Fax: 01625 524510

Information: 01625 545745
Web: www.dataprotection.gov.uk
e-mail: data@dataprotection.gov.uk

Notification: 01625 545740
Web: www.dpr.gov.uk
e-mail: mail@notification.demon.co.uk

Telephone Preference Service
DMA House
70 Margaret Street
London WIW 8SS
Subscriptions: 020 7291 3326

Complaints: 020 7291 3323

Fax: 020 7976 1886
Web: www.tpsonline.org.uk
e-mail: tps@dma.org.uk

To register a phone line not to receive unsolicited marketing: 0845 070 0707
To register a business fax line not to receive unsolicited marketing: 0845 070 0702
An on-line commercial number checking service is available at marketingfile.com

Criminal Records Bureau
Customer Services
PO Box 110
Liverpool L3 6ZZ
Information line: 0870 9090 811
Web: www.crb.org.uk

Bates Wells & Braithwaite, the solicitors whose partner Stephen Lloyd has helped with this book, are at:
Cheapside House
138 Cheapside
London EC2V 6BB
Tel: 020 7551 7777

Many organisations operating within specific sectors have done work on the application of the Data Protection Act to their constituency. The following (in alphabetical order) are among those known to the author at the time of writing.

Direct Marketing Association
DMA House
70 Margaret Street
London WIW 8SS
Tel: 020 7291 3300   Fax: 020 7323 4165
e-mail: membership@dma.org.uk
Web: www.dma.org.uk

Comprehensive guidance on how the Act affects direct marketing is being prepared, in consultation with the Home Office and Information Commissioner. When published, it will be available to non-members, but could be costly.

Institute of Fundraising
Market Towers
1 Nine Elms Lane
London SW8 5NQ
Tel: 020 7627 3436   Fax: 020 7627 3508
e-mail: enquiries@institute-of-fundraising.org.uk
Web: www.institute-of-fundraising.org.uk

The IF has published guidance notes on the 1998 Data Protection Act, £2.50 to non-members.

London Advice Services Alliance
2nd floor, Universal House
88–94 Wentworth Street
London E1 7SA
Tel: 020 7377 2748   Fax: 020 7247 4725
e-mail: info@lasa.org.uk
Web: www.lasa.org.uk

LASA has published a series of guides which includes The 1998 Data Protection Act, *8 pages, April 2000, £5.00.*

Telephone Helplines Association
4 Dean's Court
St Paul's Churchyard
London EC4V 5AA
Tel: 020 7248 3388   Fax: 020 7651 4320
e-mail: info@helplines.org.uk

The THA is actively exploring the implications of the Act for those running confidential helplines.

Training

Training courses are held by:

Directory of Social Change
24 Stephenson Way
London
NW1 2DP
Tel: 020 7209 4949   Fax: 020 7391 4808
Web: www.dsc.org.uk
e-mail: training@dsc.org.uk

A training guide is produced at regular intervals throughout the year, and up-to-date details of the training programme can be viewed on the website.

In addition, many local Councils for Voluntary Service organise training on how to comply with the Data Protection Act, and/or can give advice. If you do not already know your local CVS, contact:

National Association of Councils for Voluntary Service
3rd floor Arundel Court
177 Arundel Street
Sheffield
S1 2NU
Tel: 0114 278 6636   Fax: 0114 278 7004
Web: www.nacvs.org.uk

This site has links directly to the sites of local Councils for Voluntary Service.

Publications

The Voluntary Sector Legal Handbook, Sandy Adirondack and James Sinclair Taylor, Directory of Social Change, 2001 (2nd edition), ISBN 1 900360 72 1
A comprehensive and authoritative guide to the law for voluntary organisations.

The Fundraiser's Guide to the Law, Bates, Wells & Braithwaite and Centre for Voluntary Sector Development, Directory of Social Change, 2000, ISBN 1 900360 78 0

Information Management for Voluntary and Community Organisations, Paul Ticher and Mike Powell, Directory of Social Change, 2000, ISBN 1 900360 48 9

Other books on Data Protection include:
Blackstone's Guide to the Data Protection Act, Peter Carey, Blackstone, 1998, ISBN 185431866 7
Data Protection: Law and Practice, Rosemary Jay and Angus Hamilton, ISBN 075200 6231
Data Protection for Library and Information Services, Paul Ticher, ASLIB, 2001, ISBN 0 85142 467 8

Appendix A Limited companies and charities

There is frequently confusion among those who work in voluntary organisations which are also charities about the relationship between company registration and charity status. The following notes may be helpful.

Any organisation is either 'incorporated' or 'unincorporated'. There are several forms of incorporation, the commonest of which is a limited liability company.

A commercial company is likely to be 'limited by shares': the members of the company are shareholders. Each owns a part of the company and usually receives dividends if it makes a profit. Trading companies linked to voluntary organisations are likely to be limited by shares. Normally the shares (or single share) are all held by the parent voluntary organisation or by trustees on its behalf.

For voluntary organisations themselves it is usually not appropriate to be limited by shares. They will most likely be 'limited by guarantee'. The members in this case do not own the company, but they sign up to guarantee a small fixed amount (often £1) if the organisation cannot pay its debts when it is wound up.

Limited liability, whether by share or by guarantee, means that if the company gets into debt, the individual members are unlikely to be held personally liable for the debt. In the vast majority of cases, all they will lose is the value of their shares or the amount of their guarantee.

All companies – whether limited by shares or by guarantee – are incorporated (which literally means 'made into a body'). Incorporation means that the company has its own legal existence. It can sign contracts, borrow money and be sued, as though it was a real person. For Data Protection purposes this means that a company can have all the duties and responsibilities of a Data Controller in its own right.

An 'unincorporated' organisation doesn't exist as a legal person. This means that technically it cannot properly meet the definition of a Data Controller. The Information Commissioner has indicated that for day-to-day purposes she will normally accept Notification from an unincorporated association in its own name, and deal with it in other respects as a Data Controller. However, if it should ever come to legal action, this would most likely have to be taken against the trustees or management committee members individually.

If you are in any doubt about your organisation's status, you need to refer to the governing document. For a limited company this will be its 'Memorandum and Articles of Association'. For an unincorporated association it will probably be a 'Constitution' or 'Rules'. For a trust (a form of unincorporated organisation) it will generally be a 'Trust Deed' or 'Declaration of Trust'.

Charity status is a completely separate issue. A charity may be incorporated as a company limited by guarantee, or it may be unincorporated. The issue in either case is whether its purposes are wholly charitable. If they are, it is a charity, with all the consequent obligations under charity law, including the requirement to register with the Charity Commission in most cases. If the purposes are not wholly charitable, it cannot be a charity, even should it wish to be.

Charitable status has no effect at all on your Data Protection responsibilities, although various special provisions for *non-profit* organisations are described in the text of this book.

The easiest way to find out if your organisation is a registered charity is to look at the Register of Charities on the Charity Commission website (www.charitycommission.gov.uk.) and see if your organisation is listed. If you are still in doubt about whether the organisation is charitable – or if you think it should be registered with the Charity Commission but is not – contact the Charity Commission for further advice. Note that some charities are registered with the Inland Revenue rather than the Charity Commission. The Charity Commission can advise about this.

The Charity Commission works from three offices, in London, Liverpool and Taunton. If you already know which office covers your charity, use that contact. If not, use the national phone number, 0870 333 0123, or the website (see above).

Appendix B 'Schedule 3' *Conditions for processing sensitive personal data*

1. The data subject has given his explicit consent to the processing of the personal data.

2. (1) The processing is necessary for the purposes of exercising or performing any right or obligation which is conferred or imposed by law on the data controller in connection with employment.

   (2) The Secretary of State may by order –

   (a) exclude the application of sub-paragraph (1) in such cases as may be specified, or

   (b) provide that, in such cases as may be specified, the condition in sub-paragraph (1) is not to be regarded as satisfied unless such further conditions as may be specified in the order are also satisfied.

3. The processing is necessary –

   (a) in order to protect the vital interests of the data subject or another person, in a case where –

   (i) consent cannot be given by or on behalf of the data subject, or

   (ii) the data controller cannot reasonably be expected to obtain the consent of the data subject, or

   (b) in order to protect the vital interests of another person, in a case where consent by or on behalf of the data subject has been unreasonably withheld.

4. The processing –

   (a) is carried out in the course of its legitimate activities by any body or association which –

   (i) is not established or conducted for profit, and

   (ii) exists for political, philosophical, religious or trade-union purposes,

   (b) is carried out with appropriate safeguards for the rights and freedoms of data subjects,

   (c) relates only to individuals who either are members of the body or association or have regular contact with it in connection with its purposes, and

   (d) does not involve disclosure of the personal data to a third party without the consent of the data subject.

5. The information contained in the personal data has been made public as a result of steps deliberately taken by the data subject.

6. The processing –

   (a) is necessary for the purpose of, or in connection with, any legal proceedings (including prospective legal proceedings),

    (b) is necessary for the purpose of obtaining legal advice, or

    (c) is otherwise necessary for the purposes of establishing, exercising or defending legal rights.

7. (1) The processing is necessary –

    (a) for the administration of justice,

    (b) for the exercise of any functions conferred on any person by or under an enactment, or

    (c) for the exercise of any functions of the Crown, a Minister of the Crown or a government department.

  (2) The Secretary of State may by order –

    (a) exclude the application of sub-paragraph (1) in such cases as may be specified, or

    (b) provide that, in such cases as may be specified, the condition in sub-paragraph (1) is not to be regarded as satisfied unless such further conditions as may be specified in the order are also satisfied.

8. (1) The processing is necessary for medical purposes and is undertaken by –

    (a) a health professional, or

    (b) a person who in the circumstances owes a duty of confidentiality which is equivalent to that which would arise if that person were a health professional.

  (2) In this paragraph 'medical purposes' includes the purposes of preventative medicine, medical diagnosis, medical research, the provision of care and treatment and the management of healthcare services.

9. (1) The processing –

    (a) is of sensitive personal data consisting of information as to racial or ethnic origin,

    (b) is necessary for the purpose of identifying or keeping under review the existence or absence of equality of opportunity or treatment between persons of different racial or ethnic origins, with a view to enabling such equality to be promoted or maintained, and

    (c) is carried out with appropriate safeguards for the rights and freedoms of data subjects.

  (2) The Secretary of State may by order specify circumstances in which processing falling within sub-paragraph (1)(a) and (b) is, or is not, to be taken for the purposes of sub-paragraph (1)(c) to be carried out with appropriate safeguards for the rights and freedoms of data subjects.

10. The personal data are processed in circumstances specified in an order made by the Secretary of State for the purposes of this paragraph.

Selected additional conditions laid down by regulation

Under Condition 10 above, The Secretary of State has issued Statutory Instrument 2000 No. 417, the Data Protection (Processing of Sensitive Personal Data) Order 2000. This contains a range of provisions, including the following which may be particularly relevant to voluntary organisations.

Circumstances in which sensitive personal data may be processed

4. The processing –
    (a) is in the substantial public interest;
    (b) is necessary for the discharge of any function which is designed for the provision of confidential counselling, advice, support or any other service; and
    (c) is carried out without the explicit consent of the data subject because the processing –
        (i) is necessary in a case where consent cannot be given by the data subject,
        (ii) is necessary in a case where the data controller cannot reasonably be expected to obtain the explicit consent of the data subject, or
        (iii) must necessarily be carried out without the explicit consent of the data subject being sought so as not to prejudice the provision of that counselling, advice, support or other service.

7. (1) Subject to the provisions of sub-paragraph (2), the processing –
    (a) is of sensitive personal data consisting of information falling within section 2(c) or (e) of the Act;
    (b) is necessary for the purpose of identifying or keeping under review the existence or absence of equality of opportunity or treatment between persons
        (i) holding different beliefs as described in section 2(c) of the Act, or
        (ii) of different states of physical or mental health or different physical or mental conditions as described in section 2(e) of the Act, with a view to enabling such equality to be promoted or maintained;
    (c) does not support measures or decisions with respect to any particular data subject otherwise than with the explicit consent of that data subject; and
    (d) does not cause, nor is likely to cause, substantial damage or substantial distress to the data subject or any other person.
    (2) Where any individual has given notice in writing to any data controller who is processing personal data under the provisions of

sub-paragraph (1) requiring that data controller to cease processing personal data in respect of which that individual is the data subject at the end of such period as is reasonable in the circumstances, that data controller must have ceased processing those personal data at the end of that period.

9. The processing –

(a) is in the substantial public interest;

(b) is necessary for research purposes (which expression shall have the same meaning as in section 33 of the Act);

(c) does not support measures or decisions with respect to any particular data subject otherwise than with the explicit consent of that data subject; and

(d) does not cause, nor is likely to cause, substantial damage or substantial distress to the data subject or any other person.

Appendix C References, police checks and the Criminal Records Bureau

References

There is no legal obligation to provide an employment reference. If you do decide to provide one, you owe a duty of care both to the subject of the reference and to the prospective employer. In other words the reference must not be too good, encouraging the employment of an unsuitable candidate, nor too bad, denying someone the chance to get a job they are suitable for, nor may it give a misleading impression.[42]

To ensure you comply with Data Protection requirements, you may want to have a policy on the type of reference you are prepared to provide. This could range from not giving references at all, through a mere statement of the fact that the person worked for you between certain dates in a certain capacity, up to a full reference with comments on their quality of work and so on. Having made your policy, you should then ensure that the records you keep when someone leaves are 'adequate, relevant and not excessive' for this purpose (and any other reason for retaining them). They must also, of course, be accurate. This could mean disposing of a lot of raw material and consolidating it onto a single summary sheet.

The Data Subject does not have the right to see a *confidential* reference by means of a Subject Access request to the provider of the reference. They may, however, make an application to the recipient. This Data Controller then, of course, has to apply the 'third party' rule (see Chapter 12). If the provider of the reference is identifiable to the Data Subject, and refuses consent, and is being reasonable, then access may be withheld.

In order to avoid complications, it is good practice to specify when requesting a reference whether you expect it to be provided in confidence, and kept confidential, or to be accessible to the Data Subject.

The Criminal Records Bureau

Under the 1984 Data Protection Act some employers adopted the practice of checking job candidates' criminal records by requiring them to apply for Subject Access to their own records and provide a copy to the prospective employer. This was not illegal, but it was not regarded as good practice, since the Subject Access request could reveal information such as 'spent' convictions, which the Data Subject would normally not be required to disclose.

---

[42] For more on references see *The Voluntary Sector Legal Handbook.*

The 1998 Act makes it illegal to force anyone to make a Subject Access request once an alternative means of checking someone's criminal record is available through the Criminal Records Bureau (CRB). After much delay this eventually became partially operational in 2002 – and immediately became swamped with a backlog.

The CRB provides for three levels of certificate:

- a **basic disclosure**, also known as a Criminal Conviction Certificate. This can be obtained only by the individual, and shows only 'unspent' convictions. It costs £12, which the prospective employer may choose to refund (as some previously did with Subject Access requests). These certificates may be used any number of times with different employers.
- a **standard disclosure**, or Criminal Record Certificate. These show cautions and 'spent' convictions[43] as well as 'unspent'. They apply to occupations such as working with children or vulnerable adults, teaching, medicine and accountancy.
- an **enhanced disclosure**, or Enhanced Criminal Record Certificate. This includes additional material, including acquittals and police intelligence, and is available for a small number of jobs such as regular unsupervised work with children.

Standard Enhanced Disclosures are issued jointly to a 'registered body' and an individual. They cost £12, although the fee is waived in the case of volunteers. These Disclosures are not transferable. The registered body may be the employer or an umbrella organisation carrying out checks on the employer's behalf. Becoming a registered body with the CRB costs £300, and the registered body must follow the CRB Code of Practice. Where a Disclosure is obtained by an umbrella body it must accept responsibility for enforcing the Code of Practice on all employers using its services.

Use of disclosure information must be fair and secure, and it must not be retained after the decision has been made. The main Data Protection implication is therefore that there may be a need to record that an appropriate disclosure was obtained, but it is unlikely that any information about an employee's actual criminal record would need to be sought or kept unless other legislation (the Care Standards Act, for instance) requires the data to be held.

---

[43] Defined in the Rehabilitation of Offenders Act 1974.

Appendix D Using photographs

The use of photographs and video material raises numerous issues. Although many of these are not directly linked with Data Protection, the questions are often raised in the context of Data Protection and related policies. This Appendix gives a short summary which may be helpful. Each of the following points should be taken into account when deciding to use photographs, especially of clients, but also of staff or volunteers, or members of the public attending events.

The discussion below refers to photographs. Similar considerations apply to video material (but not CCTV; this is a separate issue on which the Information Commissioner has issued a specific Code of Practice).

This is by no means a full statement of the law. You are strongly recommended to take specialist professional advice on the issues raised here.

Copyright[44]

Copyright normally belongs either to the person who takes the photograph or to their employer (if taking photographs is one of their duties, or something they have been asked specifically to do). Copyright can be 'assigned', with or without payment. This means that the person who holds the copyright transfers their rights completely to someone else. This should be done in writing.

If you want to reproduce material for which you do not hold the copyright, you must get a licence (permission) from the copyright holder. Again, this may or may not require payment, and it may be for a single specific use, for a whole class of uses (e.g. non-commercial), or even for any use at all. There may be conditions to the licence, often including acknowledgement of the copyright every time the material is reproduced.[45]

Copyright exists whether or not it has been claimed through the use of the © symbol. Where possible, it is sensible to indicate who owns the copyright on the back of a photograph or in the caption, and the year the photograph was taken.

Where the photograph is taken

There is generally no restriction in the UK on taking photographs in public places. However, people have a right to privacy; in private places they can legitimately object to photographs being taken. It is not always easy to tell

---

[44] There is more on copyright in *The Voluntary Sector Legal Handbook* (see Resources).
[45] For example, the Web version of the 1998 Data Protection Act states:
'© Crown Copyright 1998
The legislation on this website is subject to Crown Copyright protection. It may be reproduced free of charge provided that it is reproduced accurately and that the source and copyright status of the material is made evident to users.
It should be noted that the right to reproduce the text of Acts of Parliament does not extend to the Royal Arms and the Queen's Printer imprints.'

whether a place is public or private. The more restriction there is on entry, the more likely it is to be private.

Clearly, an advice session, a training course that participants had to sign up for in advance, or a staff party would be private, but a bring and buy sale which anyone could walk into on payment of 50p might not be.

The best thing, of course, is to make sure that people know you are going to be taking photographs and give them the option of not appearing in them. That way, you don't have to worry about whether your picnic in the park is a public or private setting. You can inform people in any appropriate way: a notice in the programme for the event, a notice at the door, a public announcement after everyone has taken their places, or making sure that the photographer asks for people's permission before taking their picture.

You should of course, make sure that people know not just that photographs are being taken, but also what they will be used for, and how to avoid appearing in them.

What you use a photograph for is important. Even if taking a photograph is allowed, that does not mean you can automatically use it in any way you like. For example, you can defame someone by printing a picture of them in a situation that implies something negative and untrue about them – illustrating a story about benefit fraud, for example, with photographs of innocent people, even if you don't claim explicitly that the people are cheats.

Are the people 'identifiable'?

If any people in your photograph are so far away and their faces, clothes and 'shape' are so indistinct that they are not identifiable, there is almost certainly no restriction on what you can use it for. Equally, there are no Data Protection considerations.

However, if the people are the main subject of the photograph, and if they are closer than full length, they are quite likely to be identifiable. There may still be no Data Protection implications, if the photograph is not 'data' – i.e. is not on computer or in a structured set (see Chapter 2). Increasingly nowadays, however, photography is becoming digital, so that even a single photograph might well be data. There is also, of course, the question of whether *you* can identify them. If you can't (and have no likely prospect of ever being able to find out who they are), then the data might not be 'personal': again Data Protection would not apply.

But what if you publish a photograph not knowing who is in it? Consider the situation where photographs of your street party appear in your community association newsletter. Someone local sends a copy to a friend who has moved away. That person sees in one of the photographs their ex-partner arm in arm with someone else and this prompts them to take violent revenge. It doesn't take much imagination to see that there are circumstances when people would prefer their pictures not to appear in print, but you have no way of knowing this; assumptions can be dangerous.

You also need to be careful about using photographs without permission in case the person in the photograph has since died. It would no longer be personal data, perhaps, but the relatives might still be upset.

Artistic, literary and journalistic purposes

There is a specific exemption from fair processing, and most of the other Data Protection Principles, for 'artistic, literary and journalistic' purposes. However, the exemption only applies if:

- the material is eventually going to be published, and
- the Data Controller believes that the processing is in the public interest on grounds of freedom of expression, and
- compliance with Data Protection is incompatible with their purpose.

These conditions mean that the exemption is unlikely to apply to any use of photographs in the majority of voluntary sector publications. There will very rarely indeed be any over-riding reason to ignore Data Protection.

Commercial use

If you want to use a photograph for commercial purposes, you *must* square it with anyone in the photograph. Normally consent is obtained through a 'model release form' where the subject(s) of the photograph agree that it can be put to commercial use, usually for a fee.[46] Clearly an advertisement for a product would be commercial use, and a person whose photograph was taken in the street might be able to claim compensation if the photograph was subsequently used in an advertisement without their knowledge or consent. But what about a brochure advertising your services, or promoting your organisation? You may decide that it would be best to get a model release form to be on the safe side.

Consent

Even for non-commercial uses, it is often good practice to get consent from the subjects of photographs. If you are putting photographs on a website, this is almost certain to be necessary (see Chapter 15).

---

[46] An alternative approach is taken by the London Eye, for example, where the booking conditions specifically require you to waive any rights you may have over commercial use of photographs taken of people visiting the attraction.

When you decide that consent is necessary, you should take the following factors into account:

- Be clear about what you intend to use the photographs for.
- Be clear about *how long* you will expect the consent to last. People who are happy to be associated with your organisation now may not be so keen in a few years' time when their interests or situation have changed.
- Make sure that you get accurate information to identify the people correctly.
- Make sure that you know how to contact people in case you may want additional consent for further uses in future.
- Make sure that anyone who gives consent on behalf of someone else is authorised to do so.

Appendix E Designing databases that take Data Protection into account

When you ask an employee, volunteer or contractor to design or modify a database, you should ensure that they do as much as possible to help you comply with the Data Protection Act by building in specific features. The following is not necessarily an exhaustive list of points to cover, but may provide a good starting point.

- You must be able to retrieve and print out absolutely all the information about a particular individual easily and in a comprehensible form, in case they make a Subject Access request.
- You must build in appropriate security measures, including access controls and back-up procedures.
- Where you hold sensitive data you should think about placing this on a screen which can only be accessed by those who need to see it or, at least, which is not visible when the record is first called up and during routine processing such as mailings.
- You must be able to keep track of people who have opted out of direct marketing, and then suppress their record when you run mailings.
- You may also need to record opt-outs from disclosure to other organisations and opt-ins to telephone marketing, e-mail marketing and fax marketing.
- You should think about recording whether and how consent was given by the Data Subject for the use of their data, particularly sensitive data.
- If the database is used for more than one purpose, you probably need to record which purpose(s) were specified to the Data Subject at the time the information was collected.
- You should think about making provision to record the source of the information and any disclosure of it. This is not always relevant, but could be, especially if it is not obvious.
- You should think about how you monitor when records were created and updated, to help you comply with the requirements that information be up to date and not held longer than necessary.
- You may need to think about procedures for automatically removing or flagging information you are no longer sure about, or no longer need.
- Any database linked to the Web in any way, or designed to exchange data with other organisations, needs to take account of the restrictions on transferring information abroad.
- You may need to record whether you have told people that you are processing information about them, and why. (If not, you may need to insert the relevant statement into your next communication with them.)
- You should think about how you brief users – either on-screen, in training materials, or in printed documentation – about what the data is for, how it can legitimately be used, and who is allowed to do what with it.

Index